BEING
AWAKE

The Grand Anatomy of Consciousness

Wolin

HERE
NOW

Dedication

First of all, I would like to thank to the members of the Thursday Gathering, including Cheongang, Hwadong, Baram, Kala, Woosim, Hyunji, Bihong, for their participation in the workshop. They encouraged me to develop into words and practice the experiences I had been harboring within myself and with my presence.

Cheongang, with his deep insight, showed me that this can be delivered through practice and conversation. Hwadong took a leap into micro-consciousness through ceaseless effort, even within a limited timeframe. Baram created a loving atmosphere by always embracing all the members. Kala pierced through her own emptiness with her keen insight. Woosim grasped being integrated with all things as one right away with his incredible focus. Bihong proved that being awake can be applied to martial arts. Without them, the instruction and exercises in this book could not have been completed in such detail.

I would also like to express a deep sense of gratitude to Hyunji, for her detailed proofreading, and to my father, who has always watched me over with silent support.

Lastly, I would like to thank all the members of the Thursday Gathering and the members of Holos. They realized the need for a tool to awaken consciousness and helped me take the first step toward writing this book.

Introduction

Through what process am *I* able to perceive who *I* am? Seeing that babies do not argue their own existence, the sense of "I am who I am" must develop in the process of growing up. What process, then makes us identify with the statement "I am who I am" and believe that the sense of *I* or self is centrally important to us? How does this *I* come to *see, hear,* and *know* things?

In these questions lie both a very interesting process and a surprising illusion. First, at the root of the whole equation is the dualism of *you* and *I*. When life energy takes one of these sides, it causes an imbalance between the two. The movement that then takes place to equalize the energy difference is the phenomenon called "knowing." In other words, when a thing is seen, the *I* that sees and the *object* that is seen are separated, with more energy being directed toward the *I* and making it a center to be identified with. In this process, the *phenomenon* in which an *object* is seen, felt, and known takes place.

However, we think that we see, hear, and know. Here occurs the delusion. When we take a closer look, we come to understand that an entire network of consciousness is operating, labeling things seen, heard, and known as opposed to us actively seeing, hearing, and knowing them. Thus we come to the realization that *I* is merely one of components and that the whole flow is comprised of a pure life force. All the sensations that indicate that a separate self exist, that things exist, that noises and foods that sound or taste different from others exist are merely part of the momentary patterns created by the field of this life force.

With this book *Being Awake – The Grand Anatomy of Consciousness*, you will experience this process not by simply reading theory but through *hands-on experience*, through which you will become free from the pattern of *I* and find that you have always been in a *place* in which you can make free use of the pattern.

Wolin

November 1, 2009

Contents

Contents

THE EVENTS

The Events of Our Lives Show Us the Way.

The Events That Have Formed My Life

All organs and cells in the human body are connected as *one* through communication. Likewise, people communicate to return to an unconscious state of oneness. We do this by speaking and writing. Let me tell you a few anecdotes to do such communication. In my stories, you will see how my *existence, which had been limited by consciousness,* got over *existence as a phenomenon.*

Existence and *absolution* are just different words for *separation* and *wholeness.* When someone *exists,* it means that they are in a state of *separation* because all things that are not separated from a whole cannot exist individually, just like a wave exists only when it is separated from the water, and ceases to exist when it returns to the water. Of course, the water does not disappear once a wave falls. Therefore, it can be said that something *exists* only when it is *separated* from a whole. Surprisingly, however, this separation can be achieved only in our conceptional minds. Our *consciousnesses,* which themselves can function only through *separation,* create the separation itself.

Our limited consciousnesses makes us believe that we *exist* individually. With the discussion and exercises in this book, you will be able to see and experience how elaborately fabricated a fiction this belief is.

A Life Force Comes into Its Own When Flexible

This is a story from my childhood, when my immature competitive spirit and arrogance to get the better of others began to settle in. In fourth grade, I was playing with friends in a large factory building. We were holding a long jump contest, leaping from three-story-high scaffolding onto a big pile of sand. Greedy to jump the furthest, I stepped backward little by little to secure a longer run-up, missed my step, and fell backward. Falling from the three-story-high scaffolding to the cement floor, I hit the back of my head and lost consciousness. My friends rushed to me with fear in their eyes. One of them carried me on his back and laid me down on the lawn in front of the building.

I had hit my head against cement, but I didn't feel like I had gotten hurt. My friends all ran to me and looked down at me. With my eyes slightly open, I seemed to be fine, so, sighing in relief, they went home. After lying in the grass for an hour, I walked back home with a friend, who supported me under the arms. He was the son of the factory building's owner. And the next day, I went to school as usual and continued my daily routine.

What I recall now is that because I had no idea what was happening, I had no fear nor worry about what would happen to me while I was falling.

When there is no fear, our body is alive with flexibility. I survived back then because my body didn't stiffen in fear. We often hear news about, for example, a drunken person who collapsed on cement but ended up being fine, or a child who fell from a height and survived with no injuries. This is because the bodies of these people remained loose instead of getting stiff with fear.

Such is the case with consciousness. When we face a dangerous situation and stiffen in fear, we experience the *death of consciousness*. When is consciousness alive? When is its life force used to the fullest? The answer is when it is flexible. If you have an unyielding *I* saying, "This is who I am! I won't allow you to touch me! Things must be the way I believe them to be," you have a stiff, rigid consciousness. And a stiff consciousness will inevitably be broken. It easily becomes hurt and afraid. It gets aggressive to protect the *I*. Eventually, you will struggle with your life in the endeavor to protect rather than use your *I*, which, unbeknownst to you, is just a made-up concept. A life that is flexible is beautiful and makes room for you use your life force to the fullest.

The Peace of Warm Water

When I reached my mid-teens, my life wasn't very different from my pre-teen days. It didn't occur to me to think about what kind of life I was living. Every day was the same as usual. Then, one day, I encountered a pleasant experience. Early in the morning before breakfast, I poured warm water into a washbasin. Dipping my hands into the water, I zoned out and held them there absentmindedly, forgetting to wash my face. Especially in the winter, I would lose track of time like this, enjoying the warmth in my hands without thinking about what I was doing or having any thought at all. I would just sit and enjoy that state of being. I didn't know what this was back then. Later, I learned that I was entering a place where thoughts stopped—a kind of *salvikalpa samadi* (meditative practice) lead by warmth.

Inner separation doesn't exist in this state. Since I was a child, I've never had many thoughts nor went to much trouble to get rid of the ones I did have, so when this peaceful state of mind arose naturally, I soaked happily in it. We all experience such moments of peace when growing up, and that's why we can return to them in adulthood. The only difference is that in order to find the peace again, while keeping all our thoughts with us, we have to leap higher and higher. It is as if back then the wave was small and easily calmed, and with the calmness it was easy for the life force to move its focus from the wave to the water. On the other hand, as adults, we bear the burden of countless thoughts and emotions, which make it difficult to maintain a calm mind. Nevertheless, because we have tasted this calm water in our childhoods, or rather, because the water still causes waves of thinking in us, we can move our attention to the water again, at any moment.

If there is something that needs to be changed now, it is that we need to try to make a path from *salvikalpa samadi* (有種三昧) to *nirvikalpa samadi* (無種三昧), one that starts with the fictitious seed called the self rather than with the *samadi* that visits us naturally. With the exercises described in this book, you will be able to go from *savitarka samadi*, where you can enter into the true nature of things by forgetting their names, forms, and textures, to *salvikalpa*, where everything disappears and all that remains is the observer watching an empty mind, and finally to *nirvikalpa*, where even the observer disappears.

Emotions Can Disappear in an Instant

One of the most important incidents in my life, which I will never forget as long as I live, happened when I was completing my military service. Although it was over in a flash, this moment still exercises great influence over my attitude toward life.

I was serving in an engineering unit. One winter day, I was sent to a paddy field in Yeoju for a military operation. Our job was to lay the foundation for a temporary airfield. We were ordered to transform the huge field in Yeoju into a facility for takeoff and landing. The runway we built was not a typical one made from cement but a temporary one constructed by connecting thick, 1.5-square-meter aluminum plates to each other. We carried these plates across the frozen ground of the paddy field. The aluminum plates were too heavy for one person to carry, so we carried them in pairs. My partner was my military friend who had enlisted at the same time as me. He was a very nice person, the kind of person who would never have done anything bad to anybody. We were very close—he was my best friend in the military and had a good heart. We carried the heavy aluminum plates one by one. In such a task, one must keep in step with one's partner. If one person loses his grip first, the other person must let go simultaneously. Otherwise, we would get injured because of the weight of the metal.

While we were carrying the plates, my friend lost his grip and dropped the plate by mistake. He avoided the falling plate because he foresaw the incident, but I didn't. The aluminum plate dropped on my foot and there bloomed a tremendous pain. My thick combat boots didn't help much to soften the shock, and the cold winter weather pained my frozen foot even more. Anger flared up in my throat immediately, but I knew I shouldn't be angry with him because he didn't do it intentionally. He was not the kind of person who would such a thing on purpose.

Even so, there was no way to stop the anger in my heart. I didn't want to look at him. I walked away and kicked the ground, cooling off from my anger. You probably have experienced such anger—the kind you can neither release nor hold inside. My friend gently approached me, carefully scanning my face. He smiled apologetically. At that moment, I couldn't help but smile back.

That's the moment that something amazing happened.

Back then I had been working on looking into myself, so I was able to see my emotion disappear instantly. It seemed so surprising and wondrous to me. Such a strong anger simply vanished from my mind. The anger that had been raging in my heart like a powerful storm disappeared at the sight of his smile. It was then that I realized that anger is something that can disappear in a moment, no matter how strong it is. Since then, I haven't held any emotion for very long, and I don't let them overwhelm me.

Until then, I had unconsciously thought that anger had to be removed or resolved over a long period of time and that the person that caused the anger had to be involved in the solution. In a deep layer of my unconscious, I presumed that it was reasonable for anger to arise in such situations, that otherwise it would be a defect or a flaw in the value of my existence. I learned from that day that even without anger, my being is always perfect and flawless. This is how I learned that all emotions, including anger, can disappear as quickly as they arise.

In fact, these things happen often in everyday life. For example, you might be arguing fiercely with a family member at home when a neighbor who has nothing to do with the matter stops by. You will receive him with a smile and be kind to him, and in the neighbor's presence, your fiery anger disappears. But after the neighbor leaves, it returns. While these kinds of situations happen often, you still don't realize that anger can vanish in a moment. This is because you have not experienced it consciously.

A single realization—that is what is truly important. In fact, before this single realization, such situations had happened countless times in my life. However, I had not been aware at all, and *only after I became conscious of* the fleeting nature of emotions did my attitude toward emotions significantly change. The power of observation is incredibly important. Thus, I came to this idea: if realization can stem from everything we experience, a person's life can turn into wisdom itself.

Go Beyond the Pain of the Mind

In college, I became awakened to the feeling of intense love for the first time. My guess is whatever one's first experience may be, it is always powerful. Just touching her with my fingertips made my whole body shake with joy. When I slowly reached out my hand to touch her shoulder, it felt like literally all the cells of the body woke up and performed a cosmic dance. The nerve endings in my hand became extremely sensitive, and the moment I touched her shoulder, all my sensory receptors were so concentrated on that single touch that nothing else registered in my consciousness. It was an eternal moment. I believe eternity is something like that. I couldn't feel time, only the present moment. When I went back home after seeing her, thoughts of her filled my head, and even in my dreams, the details of my own life were brushed aside by her.

Unfortunately, this period of intensity was over before long. I could have easily forgotten it if we had parted because our feelings faded away, but we ended up parting when my new flame for her was burning the strongest, and it pained me that I could not continue to experience the thrill of joy that I had been experiencing for the first time. The bitterness and the pain in my chest were as overwhelming as the intensity of the joy had been to me, and I couldn't bear it.

In addition to her, two other things were at the center of my life at the time. One was my urgent obligation to write a thesis, and the other was my study of meditation under a teacher, from whom I always heard the phrase, "Go beyond the pain of the mind." With the addition of the pain from parting with my first love, I was undergoing triply difficult mental load.

Back then, I could not understand what this phrase meant. I

could feel pain, but how I could go beyond it? If I did so, would I feel no pain? I had no clue how to understand this phrase.

However, through heartbreak, I realized that I was bigger than *the pain of the mind*. When we are awake and consciously make it through a pain that seems too big to endure, we can understand that we are greater than *the sum of the pain* that we tend to perceive as *ourselves*."

After the breakup, I felt actual pain in my chest, and it kept me from eating and sleeping properly. It felt like all of my energy was draining out of my hands and feet. I spent days upon days feeling lethargic, zombie-like. I even skulked by a library window to watch her walk home. Stuck in the corner of the engineering college library, I spent almost three months running my eyes over my thesis over and over again, but no matter how hard I tried, my head remained empty and I couldn't absorb a thing. The pain in my chest showed no sign of alleviating. I literally did nothing but idle my time away.

Then one day, after three months, I had a truly surprising experience. It was more of a realization than an experience, actually, and it became such a turning point in my life that I felt a new sense of existence. Feeling empty and sore as usual, I was going to the engineering college library with books for my thesis paper. There were many students in the small library, tucked away in the corner of campus, and they were working hard to achieve their goals. I sat down at an empty desk and opened my book, thinking dejectedly to myself, "I am once more going to face the words that I just can't understand, just like yesterday." Then, I read one page, and another page after that, and suddenly, I was shocked. I was actually reading it! The contents of the book came into my head, the structure became comprehensible, and the plot vividly came to life on the screen of my mind. It couldn't be! I checked on the pain in my chest. The soreness was still there, and my sense of being unloved still took up space in my being, just like yesterday. But in the meantime, *the book was being read!*

I was surprised, and immediately asked myself, "Ah, is this what it means to go beyond pain?!" The pain in my heart was the same and hadn't diminished, but I could finally see the books that I had not been able to read, and *was able to do* everything else, too.

Only then did I get a clear understanding of what it means to "go beyond pain." The point was not that the pain of the mind disappears, but that you become aware that *your being is bigger than the pain.* It's like a surfer, who, afraid of a one-meter-high wave and unable to move even a single step, must be dashed into the water many times before becoming able to ride the wave with ease. It is not that the one-meter-high wave does not come, but that he becomes bigger than that wave. He no longer fears the pain from it. While I consciously felt and endured the pain for three months, the center of my being moved beyond it to a greater side.

However, the mental world is different from the surfing world. In surfing, when a two-meter-high wave—much bigger than a one-meter-high one—comes, you become afraid again and must improve your skills in order to surf it. In the mental world, you must turn to *deduction* or *insight phenomenon.* Once you firmly establish that *you are bigger than any pain*, the pain cannot shake you any longer.

This was an insight that ended my *mental suffering*. Of course, there were painful moments after that, but rooted deep in every instance of pain was a *safe peace*, a promise that *I was bigger than any mental suffering*.

The Experience of *I* and the *World* Disappearing

The reason I was wandering was not to end my pain but to taste the water of life, so I continued pursuing, hoping to figure out what had not been resolved yet. I continued practicing breath training, reading books, and attending various workshops. Eventually, I took a course on consciousness. The beginning of the course bored me, but the final stage was deep and led to some significant experiences.

By the end of the course, I was practicing erasing my thoughts. Looking within myself, I zoned in on where thoughts arose, and every time one came up, I would catch and erase it. When another thought came up, I erased that one, too, and the practice became repetitive. Interestingly, as my process of erasing thoughts became functionalized, the speed at which I erased them also began to increase. Soon, my *thought-erasing speed* became faster than the *speed at which thought arose*, and I finally came to a state in which there were no longer thoughts to erase. It was like removing furniture one by one from the room and now I'm facing an empty space.

In the empty inner space, only the *I* was felt, looking around, waiting for a *thought* to appear. Sensing this, I waited for a moment. In a flash, as if I was hit by lightning, I came to a surprising insight. It was, "Isn't the *I* that is waiting for thoughts to arise a thought itself?" When I reached this insight, my mind's automatized *thought-erasing function* began working and suddenly the *I* that had been waiting for thoughts to arise in my mind *erased itself*. I began to fall into an unknown bottomless space. It felt like what a black hole might feel like.

I and the world disappears together. Never does only one of the two disappear, because *the world* and *I* are one and the same. If *the world appears* to you, it is proof that your *I* exists somewhere that sees the world. At this moment, if you are *conscious* of something, it is proof that there already is a certain *identification* that has occurred. The identified *I* will be referred to as *gamji* (感知) in this book. That is because in the development of consciousness, we sense things purely *as they are*, collect traces of those sensations, and arrive at the feeling of *knowing*.

Anyway, while I was erasing thoughts, both the *world* and *I* disappeared together. At that moment I was neither a rising *thought* nor the *I* that was erasing my thoughts, and there was only the sense of falling into a deep black hole. It was like my entire being was being immersed in inexistence or nothingness. I lost track of time. My body shivered from cold. Someone put a blanket over my shoulders and took me out for a walk. It was not *I*, but just my feet that were walking along a hill behind a big building. There, too, were many things that were visible to my eyes but none of them registered in my mind. They just flowed by, ephemeral sensations leaving no trace in my mind. I had sight but was not seeing. There was only now. There was no past, present, or future filled with objects to *know*. That's when I realized the meaning of "*no mind, no time.*" Sensory information entered my eyes, but I *knew* nothing. No pictures were drawn in my mind. Perhaps two or three hours passed. I did not want to do the course anymore. I felt no need or desire. I left for home, saying I did not need the course anymore. Since I could not feel my *I*, how could I set new life goals for it?

I think I spent three days like that. After a few days of being in the black hole with no thoughts, I came back to the world of consciousness. Had I achieved what I had sought? I was not sure, but there was nothing I wanted anymore, so I spent another three months or so in peace, as if my feet were just floating along through the world.

This was, however, just another experience, and experiences come and go. As the experience's grip on me weakened, I began to be challenged again by my daily life. Though they were weaker than before, emotions rose again, mental desires and doubts too, and my mind began to become stained. Was this not the end?

The Eye Can See Everything but Itself

After falling into the black hole, I thought that I was done, that there was nothing more to achieve. I felt that I finally understood what the *absence of self* was. Once I fell into its deep labyrinth, an unknown and unshakably absolute nothingness refused to leave me, sitting deep in my being. After three days in this state of absolute nothingness, where there existed nothing but darkness both inside and outside of myself, I felt that my life's work was finally done. Even when I walked or ate, the black hole's sense of nothingness was with me. Inside me, there was only peace, and nothing was happening outside.

However, after about three months, the *sensation* gradually faded. Though weaker than before, I began to be swayed by my thoughts; emotions arose subtly, and the sensation of nothingness slowly faded away. It was not until then that I started to think that this was not all there was. You can deceive everyone in the world but yourself. The thought, "Not enough, not yet," came up from within me, and I couldn't stop myself from being swayed. What else is there? Was it not that I had experienced the so-called no self? Or was it that that experience was just another experience, and by nature could not last?

My mind began to travel again, skipping over the present. Then, at a time that felt right, I came across a book called *I Am That* that spoke from the perspective of *The Absolute*. I found this book very interesting because I liked the characters who asked questions. They persistently questioned the teacher in the book, Nisargadatta Maharaj, rather than just accepting answers without interrogating them. I felt that they were asking exactly what I wanted to ask, myself. And all the answers hit the spot. It reminded me of the Buddhist sutra of Nāgasena's questions and Shakyamuni's answers that I had encountered in my early twenties. Unlike other Buddhist scriptures, this one described the heated discussion between the two in great detail, distinctly different from the other ones that just revered and refused to refute Shakyamuni. Likewise, in *I Am That* the questioners kept on asking questions until they either gained understanding or an experience occurred to them, and Maharaj gave them clear answers with no hesitation at all.

But while I was reading his book, I got stuck on one phrase: "The eye can see everything but itself." It felt like I was hovering on the precipice of understanding it. It entered my heart and stayed there for days and days without leaving. Was it not that a koan should be like this? A phrase that deeply pierces the heart and does not leave, not because a teacher instills it in me but it finds me for a reason. Was it not that I intentionally tried to hold on to it, but the phrase by itself had settled in my heart and would not leave? There was nothing I could do about it. At night, I fell asleep with the phrase, and when I got up in the morning, I started another day with it. The feeling of getting it yet not really getting it, as if I was standing on a threshold, consumed me and kept me from moving along. Perhaps if I hadn't understood the meaning of it at all it wouldn't have captivated me as much. It was because I partially understood it that I knew I would fully understand it if I just took one more step—I was caught up in the words that much. I came to feel that a *koan* was not something that someone gives to a person to hold onto, but something that won't leave by itself—a *live phrase* that lives within a person. This live phrase confiscated my will and took all my energy with it.

I don't know how many days passed in this state, but I knew for sure that my whole consciousness was focused on "the eye can see everything but itself." It was my koan at the time. Then one day, finally, clear understanding flooded through my body. At that moment, it felt like everything was falling apart. It was a freedom so light that I felt weightless.

Just as the eye sees everything, so does the source of the mind see everything happening within it. This includes thoughts, emotions, underlying feelings, and everything else that is felt, known, and experienced by the mind. These are all objects, and not the true essence of self. The true me is the source of the mind, which cannot be experienced. Just like the eye cannot see itself, the source of my mind cannot see, know, or experience itself. Only the fact that there are objects (thoughts, feelings, and the like) proves that the source exists. It became very clear that the source can be described only by using negation like "neither this, nor that."

It could be taken for granted, but the impact that these words—"the eye can see everything but itself"—had on me was enormous. The part of my *mind* that had been seeking for something was gone. When a *doubt* arose, I simply felt *it* and when an emotion arose, I simply saw *it*. When the inner events of joy, anger, sadness, happiness, affection, disgust, and desire happened, I saw *it*. I could point out everything that happened inside me as *it*. Later, I found out the reason for this. It was because my *identification* with these things had been cut off. Inside, there was nothing to be called *I*. The phenomena of being swayed by, being attracted to, or resisting any given inner occurrence disappeared completely. The reason why I became to fall into my mind again after living in a void of nothingness for three months is because I turned my attention toward the experience of *having experienced nothingness.* I realized that I wasn't aware that I had fallen into the trap of identification again, because I had unconsciously been identifying with the *experience* itself, pointing at it and saying *I*.

Back then, I thought it was a very surprising experience, because afterwards, questions ceased to arise in my mind. It's not that I came to know everything, but because the notion that I had to know everything or that I was not enough disappeared. This notion disappeared because I was able to stay above all the thoughts that entered my mind. Whatever kind of thought arose, be it one of insufficiency or curiosity, it didn't matter because I did not identify with any of them. My center no longer moved into thoughts, emotions, or feelings.

When I look inside now, I never get surprised by what I see. This is because without identification, I am in this neutral state at all times. Therefore, it is neither that I got something new, nor experienced something new, nor came to know something new through this. In fact, no fundamental change happened to me. But at the same time, a revolutionary change did. Now I can immerse myself in anything that I think to be necessary, without any inner interruption and distracting thoughts, and whenever my *consciousness* is not useful, I can lay it down and *take a rest.*

Basically, I no longer fall into thought or any thought-based emotion. In other words, I became detached from thoughts. However, although I had escaped the curtain that had been literally shrouding me, in some ways this being could be said to *still be the same.*

Since then, whatever thoughts and emotions go by are not a

problem. That's because *it* is just *things that happen.* I came to be able to transcend them in everyday life. Until this change, I'd had to try to empty my mind or to forcefully calm it. But now, I do *not need to avoid the daily issues of life.* **Every time a thought arises, it is in and of itself proof of the source of my consciousness, and every time a feeling arises, it is strong evidence that proves the basis of myself, which is the profound source of the universe.**

Even before, I had looked inside myself countless times and wondered where my thoughts and emotions came from. But now, I have verified that all of those thoughts and emotions are just *things that happen.* Of course, as in psychoanalysis or treatment for mental trauma, if you dig into the cause of a thought or emotion, you will find something deep in its foundation. However, no matter how deeply buried the cause may be, the cause itself is also nothing more than an *object* that rises on the field of the source. So, what is changed? How can we hear our inner voices talking to ourselves from within us? It becomes possible only when we realize that our fundamental consciousness is always witnessing everything that rises within us.

My 15-year-long desire and frustration to seek something definite vanished at that very moment. This does not mean that I obtained *something.* Rather, it was just that the *whole process* of my mind trying to obtain something was revealed. Once I got to see the entire process, suddenly my *driving force,* my desire to seek, disappeared and I became free from the desperately seeking *I.* This is when I came to understand the true meaning of the words, "**not liberation *of* the self, but liberation *from* the self.**"

Escape from Imagination

In the early days of my training, I was always seeking something amazing, like an incredible inner experience or an ecstatic state. I had this expectation that an experience in which my *I* disappears would be unimaginable and come with enormous emotional, mental, and physical changes. Of course, when the experience came, it was in a way that *I* had never imagined. It came as a very calm silence that put an end to all my seeking.

For some people, it can come through something like ecstasy or a miracle. But such experiences are only temporary. As all (true) sages throughout human history have said, we're always in the source and can't leave even for a moment. We live in the same sea of the source at all times, both before and after awakenment, so we who seek to find the source need to look at something that hasn't changed at any moment, including before and after the experience.

Also, the aspect of discovering *it* is different from person to person. To one person, it can be a great, indescribably joyful wave, and to another it can be silent peace, and to another it can be unlimited love. However, experiences of such truth, goodness, and beauty are just phenomena through which the *source appears to a person*. The source does not have any appearance, taste, or emotion, but it reveals itself in various ways depending on the person who experiences it.

There is no truth, no goodness, no beauty. There is only the source. There are three words in India that represent the source: *sat, chit,* and *ānanda*. They mean *existence,* pure *consciousness,* and *bliss* of creation energy.

However, the source is neither existence nor consciousness nor bliss. It is something that appears according to the disposition of the person who sees it. Therefore, it can never be described in words. It only appears as a soaring force of life. So, we should not distort the source with words such as ecstasy, bliss, infinite peace, or joy. This is where beginners misunderstand and begin to be misguided.

Remember that just because someone has tasted the source through a certain experience, that doesn't mean that everyone has to experience it that way. We all experience the source in our own ways. And the color, shape, and density of each experience are so unique that no two people will have the same experience. This means that if someone claims, "You have to have this experience to see the source," they are not correct. Just keep going until your own wisdom is revealed. The path is not something that just one person can teach, and it is not that there is only one path to begin with. If someone learns under a teacher who clearly explains the student's condition, it actually will be more difficult for him to achieve awakenment until he leaves the teacher, because he is bound by his teacher's *explanation*. Wisdom is revealed when one is *perfectly free* from the *self*. Wisdom and freedom are two sides of the same coin.

Therefore, there is one thing that those who have obtained wisdom share in common; that is, anyone who has become the light of the source makes their own sound. Such a person no longer follows anyone, no longer imitates anyone, and no longer impedes anyone. He squeaks if he sees that he is a mouse, and no longer pretends to be a lion by roaring, as he did in the past. He simply squeaks and knows that it is no different from a lion's roar.

To express it in the words that are the least polluted by the shadow, the source of existence is consciousness, and when we are in it, we experience bliss. Bliss is not the same as happiness because happiness is one side of the coin that has pain on the other side. Bliss comes with freedom. Are all your inner thoughts and feelings felt as *it*? If so, you will know that you are free from them, and the *sense of separation* caused by them will disappear and you will become one with the whole.

This is the case through which one can *feel* emotional bliss. That is, when standing at a border, one sees the world of separation at his left, and he sees the world of the whole at his right. There, standing there, shivering between the two worlds, the feeling of bliss is found. Only when he belongs to *separation* it is possible to *feel* it. The reason why it is possible for him to *feel* bliss's light touch is because he is separated and whole at the same time.

While *bliss* is a feeling that can happen without attraction to anything, happiness is a feeling that has a direction—you are *attracted* to something. A happy person has a reason for that happiness, and feels like he is running toward it. Of course, if this sense of happiness grows so extreme that you feel directionless, just floating in the sense of happiness itself, that would be similar to bliss. Still, the state of directionless happiness requires a lot of energy and is thus limited. Meanwhile, bliss is a feeling that calmly vibrates without an energy supply. A person in bliss becomes one with the present moment. This is what happened to Krishna's lover, Meera. She started out happy, but the happiness became so great that she entered a state of bliss so great that she started to disappear.

A state in which you don't feel anything is close to being one with the source. This is because we are *no-thing*. Feelings of ecstasy and overwhelming joy quickly disappear, because feeling is only possible when you are in a state of *change*. In other words, you can only *feel* when you are changing from *one state* to *another*. This is because you must be identified with *one state* to *feel* another. If you feel ecstasy, it is very likely that this is an emotional by-product that occurs when your *mental state* emerges from a whirlpool of constant thoughts and emotions for the first time and tastes the *state of absence of thought*. Ecstasy is not the essence of the source. Everything you can feel, without exception, is just an inner *object* that you sense in the course of change. The source, however, is not an object.

The world of *no-thing-ness* is not difficult to recognize because every one of us lives in it all the time. I hope that the undisturbed state of peace will be thoroughly and clearly conveyed to the readers through this book *Being Awake—The Grand Anatomy of Consciousness*.

Using Consciousness

We can compare the ability to use consciousness after getting free from the *I* to using a keyboard. Before we can actually *use* consciousness, we must go through the stages of ignorance, self, and freedom.

Zen master *Seung Sahn* originated the saying, "only don't know," which means being free from all thought. To taste such a free consciousness is not to *feel* that you *don't know* anything, nor *feel* that your consciousness is completely pure, but to enter *a state* in which you truly do not know. Interestingly, when you are in this *state of not knowing*, in which you can freely use consciousness, there is no *feeling* that you do not know. If you feel that you don't know, or feel a kind of emptiness, you must still be in a duality zone, since you still *feel something*. To be able to *know* or *feel* something internally, you must be divided into the subject that feels and the object that is felt. Or you need a *fixed trace* of the object. In other words, no matter how recent an experience was, you must put it in the *past*. You can never *know* or *feel* a *present moment* that is not divided. For example, *look* into your heart now and take stock of what you feel. If you feel *loneliness*, then you're holding that loneliness like taking a snap shot and constantly acknowledging that you *feel* or *know* it. If you weren't holding onto it, you wouldn't feel it, wouldn't even know it as *loneliness*. If a feeling sticks around in your heart, like a photograph that is fixed and unchanging, it is the past, which is already dead. Only the past keeps a *constant feeling* around, and we cannot *know* or *feel* anything that does not have a fixed, *constant feeling*. If you see and feel something now, that is simply a feeling from the past that the camera of your mind took and has fixed within you. Everything we think we *know* is like that. When we feel that we *know* something, we become ruminants who constantly chew on the past.

However, when you are *awake*, entering into a consciousness that is awake to everything yet not caught in anything, only then do you stay in the *present moment*. At this stage, soon you will be able to go enter the state of *not knowing*.

In terms of consciousness, we have three states. These are the state of a child, the state of an adult whose self is established, and the state of a free person who can use the self. To compare these three states to a computer keyboard, let's say that because *a child's consciousness* has not learned how to use a keyboard and does not know what to tap, he floats vacantly over it. He's not familiar with any key, so there's no key to which he is attracted nor are there keys that he rejects. Thus, he gets confused when faced with the simple challenge of typing the letter "A," although he does not even have the self-awareness to understand that he is confused in the first place. This state is called *moha* (ignorant/foolish heart) in Buddhist practice.

On the other hand, *an adult with an established self* touches one or two keys, and although he has roughly learned the entire keyboard, his hands always *stay in a fixed resting position*. When it comes to typing on a keyboard, this means the *position* from which you can type any key at any time, although no key is immediately important to you. However, in this state, the *self* is not in this position yet, and is habitually attracted to a few *familiar keys* and resists unfamiliar ones. When a new situation arises, he gets confused, conflicted between attraction and repulsion. These feelings correspond to greed and hatred. Greed comes from an attracted mind and hatred comes from resistant mind.

A free person is always floating in this *right position*, without attraction or repulsion to any key. This floating is similar to the vacant floating of *a child consciousness* that does not know, for he is not touching any key. This is why the Bible says that a *childlike* person goes to heaven. But a free person is not a child, just a person who is *like* a child. Anyway, the consciousness of a free person is like a person who is used to the keyboard and positions his hands in the air above the middle row. His 10 fingers are ready to respond to the *present* at all times. After he presses a key, he returns to his original position so he can press another one quickly. If you compare *touching a key* to *being conscious of something*, he is always in the state of being *conscious* of nothing because he is not touching any key. Therefore, he is in the state of *not knowing*, whereas an unskilled person lets his finger rest on a key after pressing it, moving it only when it is time to hit another key. An unskilled person always has his fingers on a certain key, thus, he is *conscious* of something at all times. In addition, he is attached to what he is touching, and he is resistant against others. In contrast, a skilled person is not *conscious* of anything, as his fingers are not touching any key. He becomes conscious only when he needs to, and afterwards he returns to the right position in which there is no consciousness. In this sense, it can be said that he is usually *not conscious.* But in terms of being able to respond to anything, he is always *awake.* Therefore, *being awake* is different from *being conscious.* *Being conscious* means the state of being held in the feeling of *knowing,* a thought, or some other stimuli to some extent. On the other hand, *being awake* is being not caught in any feelings, thoughts, or mental stimuli. A man who is awake can always swim out of the so-called *sea of consciousness.* However, a man who is *conscious* is always *sunk* in the sea.

The free person's consciousness is not *conscious,* per se, but it is different from sleeping or being unconscious. He doesn't even have the feeling of *knowing* right now. Neither does he have the *feeling of vast emptiness* nor the *feeling of being in a state of pure consciousness.* Feeling emptiness or nothingness is like holding down the space bar or a shift key that does not type any letter by itself. He can keep a *hold on the feeling* of nothingness only when he is *tensed or makes an effort* to do so. But the free person's consciousness just knows, without any effort, that our true nature is absolute emptiness. He does not have any *feeling* of knowing, and at the same time he does not *feel* that he doesn't know, nor he is asleep. He is in the state of *being awake yet not knowing anything,* but ready to *use the state of knowing* at any time. This is what we call a mind of wisdom.

If you can enter the *state* of not knowing at any time, rather than have a *feeling* of not knowing or nothingness, and if you can shift from the state of not knowing to the state of knowing at any time when necessary, then you have seen the *right place* of consciousness and become it. He who has seen the right place is no longer swayed by anything, for he has no center to be shaken and does not stay on any key or in any state of *consciousness*. This is because he is always in the right place of *not knowing*.

To he who knows where the *right place* is, the *life of using* begins to unfold. He can live *using* all things, whether they be thoughts, emotions, or feelings. He will live using them freely and on demand.

Definitions of Terms

The terms used in *Being Awake* may differ from what you are familiar with, as they have been categorized through experience. These clear definitions will help you with your experience.

Gamgak (感覺): pure stimuli
To use *gamgak* (to feel something as it is)

Gamgak is what we feel when we first start using our sensory organs as newborns. Like a baby emerging from the darkness, it is a state in which one has no knowledge or insight about one's sense of self and existence. *Gamgak* here is a passive acceptance. This is similar to the *vedanā* of the four aggregates[1] of consciousness in Buddhism. It is to sense things directly, not being distorted by the *I*. To state it simply, it is pure stimuli that remain when we disassociate the feelings of *name* and *form* and *quality* from our memory to the things we see.

Gamji (感知): a restrictive feeling of familiarity or knowing
To use *gamji* (to feel familiar of and acquainted with something)

---

1) *vedanā, saṃjñā, saṅkhāra* and *vijñāna*: sensations or feelings received from form, perception, mental activity or formation, and consciousness.—Trans.

Gamji is the feeling of *knowing* something. When things that are sensed leave traces that begin to pile up within us, we are able to see things outside of ourselves through the accumulated traces. The *familiar* feeling that results is *gamji*, a kind of subtle memory, at play. Through it, things are not passively *seen*, but become objects that we actively *see* through what is accumulated inside ourselves. In other words, it is not that things *are seen*, rather, we *see* them through the accumulated traces. *Gamji* is similar to *saṃjñā* (相) in Buddhism. It is a sort of fixed past that accumulates inside us. All of the familiar feelings of recognition that are triggered by seeing objects such as watches or desks or plants or animals are *gamji*. Futhermore, *feelings* like sadness and happiness are also *gamji*. It means "to know (*ji*, 知) by feeling (*gam*, 感)." Unless it's a feeling that you have never experienced before, every feeling that you think you have felt belongs to *gamji*, which is a kind of the past. Therefore, everything that you can name is *gamji*—it is the past. *Gamji* includes not only visual things but also that which you can hear, smell, taste, and touch. If you can experience and speak about *gamji*, for example, you can understand that the answer to the question that Zen masters often ask, "Which is it that is waving? The wind or the flag?" is, "What is waving is neither the wind nor the flag. It is your mind." What this means is that you feel the *gamji* of *waving* inside you, which have accumulated over time. This is not just an old zen dialogue but actually happening in our consciousness. When we can recognize *gamji*, we can understand more deeply how our consciousness functions. Going further, there is the most subtle and highest form of *gamji*: the feeling of *I*. When you, among all the *gamji* inside you, identify with the suitable *gamji* in a given situation and feel it as a *subject*, that leads to the feeling of *I*.

All *gamji* produce pain. That's because they cause attraction and repulsion among things to occur by setting the inner feeling of *knowing* as a standard. When attraction occurs, you want to follow it, and if you cannot, a subtle pain occurs. The stronger the attraction gets, the more severe the pain gets. On the contrary, repulsion is something you do not want to follow, but if you cannot avoid it, you also feel pain. All this inner attraction and repulsion is the cause of suffering. This is called *duḥkha* (苦) in Buddhism. Therefore *duḥkha* begins at the level of *gamji*. This includes not only thoughts (想), but also images and subtle feelings that are formed before thoughts.

Gamji in *Being Awake* means feelings of *familiarity* or *knowing*. It's a state that removes a *name* or *association* to any given feeling that occurs to you when you think of, for example, *a watch*. On the other hand, *gamgak* is a state that knows no name, shape, or quality. *Gamji* are the traces left by *gamgak* (sense), proof that the relationship between them has worked, resulting in attraction and repulsion. Even when you remove the name from an object, you still get a sense of *knowing* it or its image, even if you cannot tell what it is in the absence of its name. Therefore, *gamji* is a sort of history that gives us feelings of *familiarity* or *knowing*. We're not conscious of the attraction and repulsion that result from the unconscious accumulation of *gamji* and, nor are we aware of their correlation, by which we end up being swept along. Therefore, it is no exaggeration to say that we are caught in the relationships between unconsciously stored impressions. It's common to like somethings and dislike others without knowing why, to act according to instinct and regret later with understanding why you did so. Most of our likes and dislikes happen at the level of *gamji* and, usually, we are not conscious of things at this level, so we feel that our behaviors are out of our control. *Gamji* as stored memories of experience are often called karma or traces of the past, and it is said that in order to resolve them, you must enter a deeper level of consciousness to cut your link to them. Those kinds of *gamji* include hoarded memories in your genetic and collective unconscious as well as attraction-repulsion interactions among them. However, if you are awake here right now, you can see the moment when you identify with one of your *gamji,* and cut off the life energy that is automatically poured into them, so that this identification is broken and you can get free from it. Just by being awake, you can break out of the cycle of identification any time (See the exercises "Disconnecting the Chain of Identification" on page 191).

Attention: The Transparent Energy of Life

When it comes to attention, there are automatic attention and intentional attention. Automatic attention occurs involuntarily, like when we are caught off guard by a surprising sound or an alarm. This is related to our senses. On the other hand, intentional attention occurs when you *send* attention with a certain intention.

Both types of attention can be accompanied by a force that pulls inwardly (attraction) or a force that pushes away (repulsion). Attraction and repulsion may be so subtle that you cannot register them, but adults whose *gamji* are fully formed always experience these two forces, at least unconsciously. Attraction and repulsion can correspond to *lobha* (craving or greed, 貪) and *dosa* (anger or hatred, 嗔) in Buddhism. *Lobha* and *dosa* usually refer to what happens in *one's consciousness*, but here in Being Awake, we use the terms attraction and repulsion to refer to one's inner pull and push occurring not only in the conscious level but unconscious *gamji* layer as well.

Even if you are aware of your attraction (like) and repulsion (dislike), in most cases, you automatically identify with either before you are clearly conscious of them, resulting in an energy channel that is difficult to reverse. Because energy flows into the identified mental object, you unconsciously fall into the feeling of either "I hate that" or "I like that." What is important here is that you have to get out this state first.

In the case of repulsion, when energy begins to flow in, your feelings of resistance to the unwanted situation increase. At this time, you should not give your attention to the *feeling* of repulsion, and instead direct it to the part of your *consciousness that is aware* of the repulsion. This reduces the amount of energy that flows into the feelings of repulsion and allows more energy to flow into the awakened consciousness. After that, the repulsion will naturally weaken and disappear.

The most important thing here is that you should be able to see the moment when identification occurs. When you can pinpoint that moment, you do not need to try—your consciousness will enter the state of *being awake* on its own, and energy will not be wasted. Becoming aware plays a role in changing the direction of life energy, stopping the flow of energy without having to try to stop the entire river of energy that flows into identification.

Thought and Consciousness: A Network of *Gamji*

To sum up the first three steps, we must first go through the pure *gamgak* stage and leave *gamji* (what creates the feeling of something being *familiar* and *known*, and is similar to internal impression), which are a kind of trace in our source consciousness. Then, the *gamji*, the stored traces of past stimuli, and the newly sensed information by paying attention right now are compared and contrasted, causing thoughts and consciousness inside of us.

But a thought is also a pattern of source energy. Therefore, when you start to use *gamgak* to perceive your thoughts without getting caught up in the content of them, you will inevitably look into them more closely and find out that they are the *workings* of conscious energy. Then you can see the pattern of thoughts and emotions that come and go, and even more subtle pattern of *gamji*.

To compare this to water, thoughts, emotions, and *gamji* are all a kind of wave. They each have a clear shape and are distinct from each other. But upon closer inspection, you will see that they are each an *action* of water. Finally, you will realize that this action is something that occurs and disappears. Our source is like this water. This is why it is said that at the same time that there is a world where things have form and are distinct from each other, there is another world, where things have no distinction, layered underneath it.

Identification: A Tool for *Knowing* Life

From the moment that thoughts and consciousness arise, identification with certain thoughts occurs. When this identification occurs, the *I*, the part into which the most energy is poured, become fixed, and then through attraction and repulsion towards *not–I*, the emotions of likes and dislikes arise.

For example, say a car cuts in front of you at rush hour. You get angry at once. What causes the anger is the thought, "You should not be doing that" that is stored inside you. Your *I* identify with the thought. In other words, the thought as the subject bumps against the thought caused by the situation, and the feeling of repulsion arises. What's interesting is, however, that both of these thoughts don't happen *externally*, but actually arise in your *inner world*, and when your life energy identifies with one of them, the feeling of anger becomes vivid. When you become able to not identify with a rising thought, and in this detached state see the two thoughts arise and disappear, you are a step closer to freedom.

Essentially, identification is to take the thought that, among the countless thoughts arising at the moment, is most similar to the network of thoughts that you have accepted and approved in your life, name it *I*, and make it your energy center.

Emotion: The Push—and—Pull Relationship Between *Gamji*

Depending on whether the current situation corresponds to the thought that *I* identify with, attraction (greed) or repulsion (resistance) occurs, and as the energy is amplified, emotion arises. To list the main emotions in order of intensity, lethargy or apathy, sadness, fear, hatred, anger belong to repulsion, and for attraction there are indulgence in physical pleasure, indulgence in love, and indulgence in mental joy.

Apathy is when you freeze, unable to move, and your energy is trapped. Sadness is when you can move a little bit, but can only feel passively. Then there is fear, which you want to deal with somewhat, but you cannot move in fear of getting hurt, and there is hatred, which you pour out toward your opponent, and finally there is anger, which causes you to explode.

Greed can be largely categorized into physical greed, transient greed, and mental greed. Physical greed causes you to crave pleasure, transient greed, which is often called lust, causes you to desire love, and mental greed causes you to indulge in joy.

It is good to feel and use all these emotions, but the problem occurs when you fall into them. If you see the emotions that belong to repulsion as a signal of danger and the emotions that belong to attraction as something that you can enjoy, if momentarily, you are using them well.

In order to prevent yourself from falling, you should take note of the moment you are attracted to or push away any of these feelings. You can stop the energy channel forming towards them. In fact, every emotion is caused by identifying with *gamji* and forming an energy channel through which life energy is poured, resulting in repulsion or attraction with the *gamji*. Emotions that arise through this process color your body and mind.

So, when you are attracted to or resist a thought, if you instantly notice the hidden subject thought, automatic identification with the subject thought will stop and the energy channel will not be formed. This is when you will be able to see both of the thoughts.

Being Open to the Senses

You can use the method of *Being Open to All Senses* to notice your identification with a thought or a *gamji* at any time.

For example, imagine that your body is a sensitive, vibrating one and direct your attention toward your body. Note which parts of your body are stimulated by and resonating with the sounds reaching your body from all directions. By doing so, you will be able to hear every sound from all directions. Do not fall into any specific sound but hear every single one. Usually, our attention immediately tries to find the object that made the sound or the place from which it emanated, only focusing on origin. We end up paying attention to only one of the many sounds we hear, falling into that one sound. Let's try to stop the habitual *falling*.

The same goes for vision. Look around while focusing on yourself. If your visual attention does not fall on a particular thing, everything that appears in your vision *becomes seen*. It is not that you *look* at something; rather, things are passively *seen* to you.

You can do the same with your inner feelings and thoughts. Do not fall into one of your thoughts or feelings, and instead leave your attention in your center and hold it open. By doing so, all thoughts, emotions and feelings will be *felt* as a whole. It is possible to be open to all of them without trying to *feel* or *falling* into just one of them. You can see that everything is felt, seen, and thought. Furthermore, as the feeling of being *seen* gets deeper, the *subject thoughts* that hadn't been seen by *you* because you are identified with them becomes visible. In fact, you can hardly see a subject thought or a subject feeling because it has already become part of *you*. Therefore, you need a delicate, transparent, and moderate attitude to see a subject thought that you have identified with.

Being Awake: To Be Aware of *Being*

Being awake is a state of transparent consciousness. It refers to an open consciousness without any thought or feeling of *knowing*. Usually, we are conscious of certain thoughts or feelings, and we call this consciousness with content. But being awake means being in a state of consciousness that has no content, and in this sense it can be said that there is *no consciousness* either. Still, it is a state that can respond to the present at any moment—an empty, open consciousness.

When you start to be able to sense your thoughts with *gamgak*, you will start working toward feeling a *waking consciousness that is aware* of thoughts. Being awake is to use *gamgak* to feel passively. It is to use *gamgak* to feel passively everything including consciousness, thoughts, emotions, and *gamji*. The definition of being awake is sensing them with *gamgak* as they come. And that is to be open for being awake to be possible all the time.

You might get sleepy while you are doing the exercises in this book. This is because you are in the *gamji* of *being awake* instead of actually being awake at the moment. Our consciousness's ability to imitate feelings is so amazing that it can make us feel like we are awake even when we are not. In other words, it creates many kinds of subtle impression and makes us feel them. These images are also a fixed past, not what you are feeling right now, so they make you get sleepy. Without change, consciousness falls into a doze. At this time, as those impressions of being sleepy are in the foreground, direct your attention to and feel the waking consciousness in the background.

You may experience feeling tired for another reason. This is that attraction and repulsion waste energy. Attraction comes from deeming an experience a good one and trying to replay the experience over and over again, and repulsion happens when you resist feelings such as feelings of inferiority, anxiety, and distraction. Because you waste energy on resistance and greed, you feel tired. At these moments, you just need to recognize your internal attraction or resistance to something to return to the state of being awake.

Awakenment: To Realize the Nature of Consciousness, To Remain That Which Feels

Awakenment means that you remain *that which feels*. In other words, you exist as the source. It is not that you feel waking consciousness or pure being but that you stay as *the Unknown* which makes it all possible.

CONSCIOUSNESS

Consciousness is a flow and a process.

An Anatomical Chart of Consciousness

The exercises in this book are as follows: understanding the nature of consciousness, practicing attention, discovering *gamji* and *gamgak*, and finally, being awake. This process goes in the reverse order of the process by which *consciousness* unconsciously or automatically arises.

Pure sensations leave traces of *gamji* in you, and as they get your attention, *consciousness* occurs. This occurs in the order of *gamgak*, *gamji*, attention, and finally consciousness. In Buddhism, this is called the four aggregates of clinging (受相行識). *Vedanā* (受) is pure sensory input. *Saṃjñā* (相) refers to images accumulated inside oneself through sensory input, or the names given to these images. They are all the past. *Saṅkhāra* (行) is the will or action to identify something, and *vijñāna* (識) is the consciousness that results from this identification. *Consciousness* that involves feelings of familiarity or knowing occurs through this process of the four aggregates of clinging or, in our case, the process that goes from *gamgak* to *gamji* to attention to consciousness.

So we will look at them in reverse order. We will start by looking at the process from the occurrence of *consciousness*, you'll understand and experience what *attention* is, then you'll learn, experience, and distinguish *gamji*, and then, finally, you will practice *gamgak*. When you can use *gamgak* to see all things as it is right now, not as you remember it was, you will be able to *be awake*.

Some of the exercises in this book involve practicing wisdom that allows insight to arise after you calm your mind. When internal confusion occurs, it would be good to practice focusing on a bland thing before returning to the insight exercises, because confusion means you are caught in either attraction or repulsion.

There are attachment (*raga*) and aversion (*dvesha*) in Buddhist terminology, and when we look them in a more neutral way and in the aspect of energy, we can call them attraction and repulsion. The words attachment and aversion easily conjure emotions of likes and dislikes, along with all sorts of judgements due to the many images and feelings that have been attached to them since they were coined, so I changed them to the slightly more neutral terms attraction and repulsion.

Consciousness is accompanied by a feeling of *knowing*, which occurs only when there is an object and always results in the feeling of *I*. In other words, *I* and an *object* always happen together and cause the phenomenon of *consciousness*.

Consciousness occurs when we pay *attention* to something. Only when our attention reaches its object does the phenomenon of *knowing* happen. When attention stretches out so that it is not focused on one thing, you are close to being awake. At this moment, you are not conscious but awake and embrace everything. You can understand this through the previously mentioned analogy of the keyboard. Being awake and being conscious are very different things. In the state of being conscious there is conscious content into which you fall. In the state of being awake there is no conscious content into which you fall. You are simply open to the moment. Just because there's no content for you to fall into doesn't mean that you are asleep. You can tell that you are awake if the fundamental quality of your consciousness has not changed. This means it is pure not influenced by any conscious content. In order for the state of being awake with wisdom or insight to lead you to awakenment, allow me to help you.

Why We Try to Locate the Root of Consciousness

We always have to have a purpose in order to move. Humans don't move without something driving them. Modern people strive to accomplish things rather than go into eternity where *I* disappears, by being attracted to the majesty, charm, or beauty of nature. Achievement is manifested as a thought that is 'for the sake of something.' The thought becomes a motivator that makes us move. By putting your energy and drive behind a thought, you deem thoughts important and rely on them to move. Take a look at the contemporary times. Don't people claim that the power of thought is important? We literally live in an era of knowledge and thought. "Dream it, be it." "Your fate is in your hands." However, a person can become dragged down by thoughts rather than handle and use them. This is because, ironically, such a person has experienced the reality of "Dream it, be it" and has still not actually learned how to think freely. This is because he doesn't look into where his thoughts and desires come from and, believing that he thinks them on his own, falls into them. Having fallen into his thoughts, he then makes every effort to fulfill them, although they have only come to his mind at random. For example, perhaps he makes up his mind to be rich. He thinks that in a few years, he will make a million dollars. He believes that this thought is original to him, an action done by him. Did he think the thought, however? Or was it the thought that came to him? It is very important to distinguish this.

Why did he come up with the thought? Perhaps he had lived in poverty. He could have struggled with money, or compared himself to others and found himself wanting be like them. Or perhaps he set himself the lofty goal of building an equal society by rebelling against his current social situation. In any case, every cause for thought is external. That means there is always a reason, a factor, an influence. But he identifies the thought that came to him from the outside *as his own*. Driven by this thought and incognizant of its external cause, he puts all his energy into it to achieve his goal.

But what really happens then? He continuously meets obstacles on the way toward his goal. Nothing turns out the way he thinks it will. Why? It's because he is a person who, *driven by thoughts*, becomes obsessed with and blindly follows a thought that has simply *arisen* in his mind. Thus, it is hard for him to ignore all the other thoughts that pop up as well. If he had come up with a thought himself and moved on his own as a master of the thought, he would not be dragged down by the different thoughts occurring to him but would adhere to the thought he set as his goal at first. However, by chasing a thought that did not originate from himself from the beginning, he became a slave to it. This is why not all you think comes true. To be able to make things happen as you think, you, yourself, need to be free from thoughts and be able to handle thoughts. Similar to getting off on the wrong foot in a new social interaction, a person can never operate according to the Law of Attraction. Those who do must be possessed with a desire that is strong enough to silence all other thoughts, or be the rare kind of person who has unknowingly learned how to live free from all thoughts. He who can carry out a thought he had once has gained the power to defeat the many other thoughts that will come to mind in the process.

But these instances *happen* involuntarily, so it cannot be said that such a person is truly free from thoughts. Being truly free from thoughts is a precondition for the phrase "Dream it, be it" being able to actually come true. In order to be free from thoughts, you need to see their root, the source of consciousness, and manifest them yourself.

We live burdened by the concept of *freedom*, which, ironically, we ourselves created. Only humans think of freedom. Do the freely blooming flowers in the fields seek freedom? Do animals? They are free without the idea of freedom. Only we humans are confined by it, having made it ourselves. So, it is only when we go back to the source of a concept or thought that we can see its root and free ourselves from it. Then at last, for the first time, one can handle and use thoughts.

Once free from your thoughts, you are set free from your emotions as well. This is because you learn what it is to *be free*, and also because emotions originate from the same source that thoughts do. Once you see this source—no, actually, it's better to say that you are the source, because the word "see" implies that the one that sees and the one that is seen are separate beings. Once you are the source, you will no longer be confined by any thought or feeling.

Now, what does it mean to be free from thought? First, it means you can feel and see your thoughts. In order for you to use any tool at your will, you must not identify yourself as the tool. Let's take a hammer as an example.

We don't feel any sense of ourselves in a common hammer. As with any object, we do not feel that the hammer is any part of ourselves, seeing it with a sense of distance. You can take it out and use it whenever you need it and put it back in its drawer when you don't. You are not driven by a hammer. It doesn't show up from time to time and hit or bother you. Nor do you ever tightly grab a hammer once and find yourself unable to let go of it. A hammer doesn't make you happy or emotional. And of course, a hammer does not show up and tell you what to do or what not to do with your life.

Now, let's replace the word "hammer" in the above passage with the word "thought." If you feel that the above statements are all correct, then you are free from thought and well on your way to the source.

Second, what you should aim to achieve through the exercises in this book is the restoration of your natural ability to see things as they are. Everything we see is covered with images. Look around the room where you're sitting right now. Everything, living or not, possesses the *feeling of knowing* by which you name or label things. Even though you don't know the name of a thing, if you find a feeling of *familiarity or similarity* in it, you see it now through the images of the past you keep within yourself. In this way, you don't see an object as it is at any given moment. It is important to recognize this first. Let's begin our first exercise by committing to the words, "I do not see things as they are."

When you recognize that you do not see things as they are, you have taken the first step. Now, all of your energy can be focused on asking what it means to be as something is. The more eager you are, the more energy you can direct into this question. So, what is it for something to be as it is? First of all, at the very root of this, things are sensory matter. They are sensory feeling. We are no longer sensory people. Modern people don't know what it means to be *sensory*. We have become conceptual and imaginative. When we see something, our immediate thoughts are along the lines of pretty, cool, good, ugly. Or perhaps yellow, cold, mild—but all these expressions that come to our minds are concepts. To put it simply, these are *thoughts*. What comes before those thoughts are *gamji*. *Gamji* are not emotions. When a baby is born into this world and opens up his eyes and sees things for the first time, what comes to him is sensory feeling. It is what he senses, what he hears when he opens his ears for the first time. When he reaches out his hand and touches something, what he feels is its tactile sensory feeling. *Gamji* are literally what one sees when they first open their eyes.

In fact, every time we encounter something or some events, we go through the process of seeing and perceiving them for the first time. Every time you see something, the process of *initial recognition*, seeing something for the first time, passes instantaneously. Only after this process do you recognize it as "tree" or "stone." But the *initial recognition* process passes so quickly that you do not notice it. It's like driving a car, unconscious of your actions.

This is why we need to distinguish *gamji* (similar to sense) as a base. *Gamji* are a little different from *gamgak*. *Gamgak* (similar to feeling) happen first. After that, *gamji* form as traces of *gamgak*, resulting in names and thoughts arising from their interactions with each other. Therefore, the first thing you need to do is to practice recognizing and rediscovering *gamji* and *gamgak*. To do so, we will first learn to recognize *gamji* and practice consciousness development in reverse order to eventually reach sensory feelings over the course of this book.

What we call *gamgak* are not *feelings*. Feelings you can easily call good, bad, cold, warm, vague, dark, and so on. But they are thoughts, and you'll soon realize that what comes before thoughts are the *gamgak* that we are talking about here. You can learn this only through hands—on practice.

What Happens When You Are in the State of *Gamgak?*

When you can use *gamgak*, you can walk freely through the world of *gamgak*, the world of *gamji*, and the world of thought. This is because you have clearly seen each of these worlds. Of course, they are all inseparable, like the colors of a rainbow. Dividing them may in itself create more separation. However, people in primitive times only saw three colors in the rainbow, and this disadvantaged them in that they didn't use color as freely as we do now, as we consider the rainbow to contain seven colors. As such, for the exquisite *use* of consciousness, we need to subdivide the process of consciousness development.

How Does Consciousness Arise?

How does consciousness—the feeling or thought of *knowing*—occur? As we have seen, we go through four basic steps to reach consciousness. First, we use *gamgak* (感覺) through our sensory organs. What we use *gamgak* for leaves traces inside of us and results in a familiar feeling. We call this *gamji* (感知), meaning to know (*ji*, 知) by feeling (*gam*, 感). *Gamji* include feelings, images, subtle imaginations, and thoughts. When *gamji* pile up, we try to use them to identify external sensory stimulation. Then, we use intention or attention to recognize the stimuli, and consciousness occurs in the form of a feeling of *knowing*. Thus, consciousness occurs through *gamgak* (input of pure sensation), *gamji* (accumulation of *gamgak*), and intentional recognition through attention. In this book, we will practice this in reverse order, going from consciousness to attention to *gamji* to *gamgak* (識-行-相-受), in order to return to the original state of pure sensation. In this state of pure sensation, there is no consciousness, no feeling of *knowing*, and thus the feeling of *I* disappears as well, because *I* is a phenomenon that only occurs in the relation of a subject *knowing* an *object*.

Where Does Sense of *I* Come From?

What is first to be learned through self—observation is that there exists a *feeling* of *I*. This is often also called the feeling of *I am*. However, we usually take the *thought* of *I* as ourselves, not distinguishing the *feeling* beneath it. We tend to leave a simple and plain yet core experience that hits right at the spot behind, caught up with so many ideas and theories out of vanity. But what is truly important is to see through the depth of that experience, that is, to see through the essence of the experience that is from the thought of *I* into the feeling of *I am* and then into *being*.

While wandering around trying desperately to reach this essence, sometimes we come across a sage word of wisdom or classic phrase and make up our minds to find our true selves. However, the thought of *I* always disappears when you try to do so, because thoughts come and go. After spending years searching, in the right place and at the right time, you will finally hear your inner voice telling you to look into your existence. And finally, you will find the *feelings* that hold up your thoughts. Therefore, a person who wants to see the root of their own self should pay attention to their feelings rather than their thoughts because every thought comes from the feeling beneath it. Once you accept it, you will be able to look for the feeling of *I*.

If you ask yourself where your *I* is, either out loud or in your heart, you will not be able to find it anywhere but in the body. If you sit still and search inside of yourself, you will find the *feeling of being alive*. This feeling does not disappear unless you are dead or unconscious. So, when you look into your self and focus on *being alive*, eventually and without fail, you will find the feeling of *I am*.

At first, it is felt as a feeling of *I am*. When you find the feeling and decide to investigate it more deeply, gradually the *I* will disappear and only *am* will remain. This is because *I* is based on the premise of an *object* that acts as its counterpart, meaning that if there were no object except for one's own self, the *I* would disappear. If you were stranded on a desert island where there are no familiar things to speak to, no human companions with whom to share feelings and thoughts, you would have no *I*. In a space where there is no *object*, the *I* collapses and disappears. Of course, if you treat your thoughts and emotions as *objects*, that means there are inner *objects* with which you can manifest the *I*. But when you leave behind all external and internal objects and focus solely on *I am*, something interesting happens. Unlike usual observation in which your *I* thinks or feels an *object*, because you are considering yourself as an object, no separation remains between *I* as a subject and *I* as an object. What this means is that your *I*, focusing on *I am*, gradually disappears until only *am* remains.

At first, questions or feelings that accompany the thought (such as "Where am I?") become the *object*. So, it will feel like there are two things: *I* and the *object*. However, since they are actually not separated, they will gradually dissolve into each other and you will feel only a sense of *being*. It feels like you are throwing a net out, except the net is covering you from the inside. It is at this moment that you first escape the boundaries of subject and object. This is the state of being without inner separation of which Jiddu Krishnamurti spoke. He described nature in the form of a diary, expressing a state in which separation disappeared: for example, when we are overwhelmed by nature's majestic beauty and both our inner observer and the object of observation disappear. He portrayed this observation in a serene style.

We often experience the disappearance of *I*, such as when our attention is fully immersed in a thing, an event, or an object, and all of our energy pours into the constant changes of it. We suddenly leap from *I* and disappear into the thing or the event. That is what Mihaly Csikszentmihalyi calls flow. But it doesn't really help those of us who intend to see the whole process because in these cases, we realize that there was no *I* only after the moment of flow. We need to notice the entire process in real time.

In general, in order for things in the external world to be distinguished from one another, there must be space for separation between the two. The same goes for our inner world. The feeling of "I am not that" acts as the *space* that allows for us to distinguish between this and that. Thus, in situations when it feels like we are spatially separated from an object, we feel that we're objectively observing our inner world. But this also causes internal *division*. We feel that *our inner world* is separate from *that which observes* the inner world. In other words, the *intention* to observe divides our inner consciousnesses into *observer* and *object* of observation. Though you will come to understand this little by little, what is interesting here is this: in the external world, in order to distinguish this from that, *space* is needed, and in that space *this* and *that* appear together. Similarly, in the inner world, when the *observer* (*I*) and the *object* (*it*) of observation are divided, both of them appear together in the inner *space*. We usually think we observe inner objects, but we overlook that the *self* is a kind of object, too. If you feel angry, you think it is your *I* that is experiencing *anger*. But in fact, both *I* and *anger* are what appears in your inner space. *I* is an *object* from the perspective of the source, only because the center of energy is directed toward it, it feels like a subject. This is why Krishnamurti used the term internal *division*.

Sometimes we experience temporal division without spatial division. This is a common experience. Let's say, for example, you are angry for some reason or another. When the anger subsides a little bit, we think, "Oh, I got angry." Depending on the time, we feel that we are either *I* or an *object*. After the moment of anger has passed, we simultaneously feel weak traces of the anger and the feeling of *I*. Similarly, thoughts can also often be clearly distinguished from one another only through temporal division. This is because in order to distinguish between thoughts clearly, we should focus on them singularly, one after another. If you think two thoughts at the same time, you will find that it feels a bit blurry.

Anyway, how are the thoughts or images that we see as objects related to *I*? Interestingly, they involve the feeling of *I*: a feeling that says, I think of it. When *gamji* (objects) are formed in the inner space, *I* appears with them. So, *I* and *objects* appear at the same time. The reason we don't feel *I* when we are immersed in flow is because the energy that is poured into the event is so intense that it moves through it very quickly, so there's no time or space to feel *I*.

On the other hand, the disappearance of *I* that follows the feeling of *I am* is a little different from the disappearance of *I* while immersed in flow. When you feel *I am*, you experience the disappearance of *I* while being constantly aware, unlike when you disappear and momentarily immerse yourself in flow. It is different from being immersed in flow, during which you cannot be aware of the disappearance of *I*. Immersion in flow means to fall into and become one with it.

Of course, when you feel *I am*, you can still find the feeling of *I* and become one with it. However, you will always be aware of *I* because the object of immersion is not external but *I* itself. The interesting thing about consciousness is that when the subject (*I*) and its *object* are the same, they melt into each other and disappear, but being awake remains. So when you focus on *I am*, a certain waking state of being conscious of the subject occurs, unlike in the case of flow in which *I* disappears, immersed in the object thoughts, and even when the feeling of *I* disappears, the state of being awake is carried over to the state of *being*, which is the essence of the subject.

A neurobiologist is making a ceaseless effort to find that which physically correlates to the smallest unit of *consciousness*. However, it would be faster to find the *process* that enables *consciousness* rather than identify its physical components. This is because the consciousness of *I*, consciousness of *you*, and consciousness of *knowing* something are all a sort of *process* that occurs when there is an *object*, not a physically *fixed thing*. And more importantly, we should be focused on the *source* that makes the process possible.

The Birth of Consciousness

Without *I*, there is no object. If you look at a plant in front of you and recognize it as a plant, it is the *I* that is *conscious* of the plant and makes it become an object. But when the *I* that *knows* the *plant* disappears, there disappears the *plant*, too. In fact, there are no individual beings such as plants or animals in this universe. It is only the act of consciousness that makes us feel and conceptualize things as individual. Consciousness is composed of a subject and an object, and the feeling of subject and object forms a pair of maps on the screen of empty consciousness. So, when the *knower* disappears, of course the object disappears as well.

Or, the other way around, when there is no *object*, there is no *consciousness* that is *knowing* or *feeling* something, and therefore the *I* that *knows* disappears. In other words, if our feeling of an object (*gamji*) as a *plant* disappears, then so does *I*.

Thus, the feeling of an object is inseparable from *I*, so when *I* disappears, the world disappears, and vice versa. This is why someone who practices the meditation technique of becoming one with an observed thing might experience the disappearance of himself, or another practitioner of meditation who inquires into

I might at some point see that there is no *I* and experience the disappearance of *external things*.

This explanation is, of course, very delicate. Now we return to talking about *gamgak* and *gamji*. *Gamgak* is sensate acceptance of what comes before the whole is divided, without a subject and an object, and *gamji* refers to the stage that is right before consciousness and the division and conceptualization of the indivisible whole, which have been named as if they were separate.

In other words, *gamgak* are what a baby feels when he is born and first sees or touches things. The baby does not have any thought or feeling of *knowing* because there he has no image or experiential feeling stored inside. Therefore, he doesn't separate what he sees into *identified things*. Everything that he sees is just one whole that is melted into each other. When you use *gamgak*, the universe feels like an inseparable single mass or non-dual, with everything that we see as separate wiped of meaning. We call this feeling of not knowing *gamgak*. However, when we become adults and gradually store traces of the many things we have experienced and seen, *this* and *that* become separated through feelings of recognition and familiarity. The feelings of *knowing* or *recognition* that arise occurs through *gamji*, which are stored traces of the past. Distinguishing *gamji* and *gamgak* experientially is the most essential skill for being awake. When you can distinguish the two, your consciousness will have become sharp and you will be able to see the *I* and the *world*, stained with *gamji*, in a new way. From there, you will enter the state of being awake and experience simply *being*.

We have essentially two kinds of consciousness: everyday waking consciousness and subconsciousness (automated subconsciousness, vast subconsciousness, whole consciousness). If you understand that subconsciousness is truly present at every moment, you will find that a very broad spectrum of *I* is possible.

Anyway, if there are two levels of *I*, the *disappearance of I* happens at both the levels of shallow surface consciousness and deep subconsciousness. A seemingly low level of consciousness does not mean that the experience of *no self* gets less meaningful. It is important how this affects one's existence. Like a line of dominos, it falls from this surface and is transmitted to that deep layer. Because it is not that all consciousness, from the surface consciousness to *Alaya-vijnana* (the storehouse-consciousness) in the deepest layer, are separated, but that the one-time instance of *falling* happens in every dimension. That is, when we use *gamgak* to see objects, the *disappearance* of *I*, the separated individual, happens in every dimension. And as you expand and deepen this experience, you'll gain insight into what the disappearance of *me* is and where it happens.

Since ancient times, pure consciousness has been compared to light. When light is shed, *I*, *object*, and *knowledge* between the two rise. In Buddhism, it is said that *indriya*, *viṣaya*, and *vijñāna* (根境識) occur at the same time. The external object is *viṣaya* (境), the sensory organ that senses it is *indriya* (根), and the knowledge that results is *vijñāna* (識). These three things always happen together.

In other words, when you see an object (境) with your eyes (根),

awareness of it (識) occurs. The same goes for auditory, gustatory, tactile, and olfactory objects. There's one more, as well: the mental object, or thought. When you see a thought (境) with your mind (根), knowledge (意識) of it occurs.

Put simply, you can say that *I* and *object* occur together and result in a feeling of *knowing*. So when the light of pure consciousness sends attention to an external thing, you become aware of it and recognize it, and when the light shines internally, you become aware of and feel things inside.

But this prompts questions about *knowing*. When you say you *know* something, what you mean is you have compared external sensory stimuli with the traces of the past you keep *inside* you, which results in the feeling of knowing. Therefore, *knowing* always occurs through a comparison between *what exists* and *what is newly sensed*.

So, in order to say you *know* something, there must always be something accumulated inside of you to compare it with. We call the inner accumulation *gamji*, which means to know (*ji,* 知) through feeling (*gam,* 感). When a baby is born and sees things for the first time, he sees without the feeling of *knowing*, rather *realizing through feeling at the moment*, which we call *gamgak* (感覺). The difference between using *gamji* and using *gamgak* is that using *gamgak* involves no thought or feeling of *knowing*. Of course, *gamgak* is a kind of *knowing* in the sense that it *is felt* in any way. But it is clearly different from terms like cold or warm that are usually used in society. Remember, when we say using *gamgak* in this book, we refer to using a primitive sense of stimuli that is not influenced by anything. A practitioner once called it "bare feeling," like bare foot or bare hand, in the sense that it is a pure feeling that is not informed any image or emotions from the past. Of course, the true meaning of this word can be understood only through *experience*, but I will explain it as much as possible in words. Then, I hope you will learn by practicing yourself.

So how does using *gamgak* differ from using *gamji*? It is to instantly *realize* that there is a *feeling* without *knowing*. There is no *thought or feeling* of *knowing*. Whether it is tactile, visual, or auditory, you feel the *stimulus* but don't *recognize* what it is. Although, we can say that *stimulation* is a type of *knowing* itself in the sense that it is felt. Then how does this kind of knowing come about? It comes from *standardization* carried out by the sensory organs. For example, dolphins and bats emit ultrasonic waves, the frequency of which alter when they hit objects. The dolphins and bats then perceive the object through an interference wave that is formed when the original wave that they continue to send meets the altered wave. The standardization of our senses can be compared to a kind of continuous vibrating wave, like the 150,000-hertz ultrasonic wave that a dolphin sends out. The constant wave is the *standard*. However, when *gamji* (感知: 相) pile up inside, we replace our sensory wave with the images (相) we collect inside of us. This is a *gamji* wave, which sometimes causes us to perceive things mistakenly, such as when you mistake a rope for a snake because you send out the image (相) of a snake to recognize it.

So, we consider these sensory *limitations* that we are born with as a minimal standard for *existence* for having a physical body. And we see *gamji* as the cause of all anguish and suffering.

As human beings, the first thing we feel when we are born is the feeling of *existing* or *being*. This feeling is installed in the sea of our life force, which means that the feeling of *being* is constantly flowing. When *gamji* are accumulated there, a common extraction concept called *I* is formed, which turns into *I am*. This continuously flows roughly in your consciousness and subtly in your subconsciousness. When an event, object, or stimulus comes along and causes interference, a new *feeling* occurs to your *I*. The *I* that we feel is a kind of *consistently vibrating net* and when a visual stimulus comes to it and shakes it, *feelings* of, for example, *a house* occurs. If an image of a house that you once saw is stored, you will compare the visual stimulus to the stored image and the feeling of *knowing* that what you're seeing is a house occurs secondarily.

The first thing that comes before all feelings is *being*, which can be said is like a sense of presence. When we hold onto the feeling of *being*, we feel a calm peace. Like a home to which you can return and rest anytime from a busy day of working, *being* is a *feeling* that brings peace. It is like the root of existence.

So far, we've looked at *consciousness*. Now we're going to move on to exercises to practice in the order of attention to using *gamji* to using *gamgak*, through which we will gradually discover the feeling of *being*. Next, we'll go further and experience what *being awake* really is. Finally, we will find enlightenment on the source of existence and consciousness, where being awake truly happens.

ATTENTION

Being awake enables you to remain in an awakened state, resist falling into the experiences of daily life, and live by using the life force given to you by nature. It means achieving inner peace in the overwhelming whirlwind of all appearances and riding on the powerful flow of life while experiencing all its mysteries.

Types of Attention

Attention is amazingly diverse. It can be sent off inconsistently, like casting blips one after another, or it can be sent continuously, like a line. It also can work three-dimensionally, surrounding an object. When the factor of time is added to attention, it takes even more diverse forms. When look into it deeply, you will find two elements: the intensity of attention and the pattern of attention. The pattern of attention is classified into four categories.

Because all things in the universe have the same origin, they all share the same properties. Put in another way, it is called fractal structure. A part of the whole contains the whole itself, as does the whole also appear to be just a part, and parts resemble each other. The same goes for consciousness and matter. Just as a material photon is a wave and a particle at the same time, consciousness is like a kind of wave, so possesses a universal wave nature, and when it concentrates on one place, it becomes a particle. When a person, having sensed you staring at him, turns and looks at you, it is because your consciousness's wave spread, turned into particles, and somehow touched him. In this way, our consciousness can travel across space, as well as time. This is because time and space are one continuum.

We can also direct consciousness strongly in one direction, like a laser beam, or project it in all directions to resemble a big bell in a Buddhist temple to *touch* everything around us. That's what attention and concentration are in neurofeedback practices. Attention spreads in all directions, becoming conscious of the whole, and concentration makes it possible to focus the power of consciousness on one object like a laser. Let's look at the nature of attention as a basic element of consciousness.

There are four main types of attention: First, automatic attention, which is the kind of attention that is unknowingly caught by something. Automatic attention is what occurs when you suddenly hear a loud explosion from behind you and reflexively turn to look at it. In this process, first, your attention heads to the space called *behind*. This is called automatic space-oriented attention in neurophysiology. We use the second kind of attention to identify *what* the origin of the sound was. We call this automatic object identification attention. The next two kinds of attention are called intentional attention. They occur when we look at something with an internal intention. The third kind of attention is intentional space-oriented attention, which is when we intentionally pay attention to a space in a certain direction. This is the attention you use when you are, for example, about to look *above the desk on your left*. The fourth is intentional object identification attention, which is used to identify an object. When you try to identify an object, you look at the object with a certain image or feeling (*gamji*) that you refer to like a standard in your mind. For example, if you hear the sound of a coin falling onto the floor, you will look toward the floor with the image (a kind of *gamji*) of a *coin* in your mind. Intentional object identification attention is the kind of attention that you use in this case. Here occurs consciousness. So, the consciousness of *knowing* occurs the moment that you try to *identify* something external to yourself with *intentional attention* through the use of your internal *gamji*. Every state of consciousness requires you use both *gamji* and *attention*, which, depending on whether the attention is automatic or intentional, results in either the consciousness of *knowing* or the consciousness of *not knowing*. This process operates through the *skhandas* (*vedanā* · 受–*saṃjñā* · 相–*saṃskāra* · 行–*vijñāna* · 識) in Buddhism. Through *vedanā* · 受, which we call *gamgak*, the image unit *saṃjñā* · 相 (*gamji*) is formed inside yourself, and when you try to use *saṃskāra* · 行 (attention or intention) to look at something by using the accumulated *saṃjñā*, *vijñāna* · 識 (consciousness) occurs.

In summation, there are four kinds of attention: automatic space-oriented attention, automatic object identification attention, intentional space-oriented attention, and intentional object identification attention. And the consciousness of *knowing* is mainly caused by number four, *intentional object identification attention*.

EXERCISE 1.1

This attention exercise aims to help you experience and distinguish the four kinds of attention, with 10 different levels of intensity for each kind. When you can distinguish the various aspects of attention that occur within you, you will be able to identify a mental energy that is *attention*. When you can feel it, you can separate it, and from then on, you will be able to become free from identifying with *attention*. Then you will finally be able to grasp the *source of consciousness* that makes attention possible.

Ironically, we need a very fine sense of discrimination in order to return to a *state before separation*. We can only enter a world without discrimination through discrimination. First, you need to look into yourself very closely and differentiate between every detail of what happens there. Gradually, the center of your being will move away from *attention* itself toward the source that makes *attention* possible. Being immersed in attention is flow. But if you have fallen into attention, you can't grasp it. Therefore, you should not fall into anything.

Fear and anger, in particular, make the phenomenon of *attention* impossible. In other words, attention does not work when influenced by fear. If your company were to become suddenly bankrupt due to the fluctuations of a rapidly changing global economy, you might be angry, thinking that you have no control over the situation, or be daunted and fearful, imagining the difficulties to come. Would you be able to pierce this anger and fear through the use of sharp attention? Of course not.

Therefore, if you practice this attention exercise in a safe place and time, you will develop the mental muscle in charge of your *attention* and be able to use it even in times of mental anguish.

Neurophysiology says that there are four types of attention. First, there are the two kinds of automatic attention—automatic space-oriented attention and automatic object identification attention—

both of which involve the involuntary engagement of attention, hence, automatic. When an unexpected event happens and we register it with our senses, we pay automatic space-oriented attention toward the space where it happens, and automatic object identification attention to check what it is.

Let's say you are reading a book in a quiet place and suddenly hear a loud banging sound of something bumping outside. You unconsciously move your attention toward the direction of the sound. The same goes for something cool that catches your attention, something that looks weird, a fragrance that you haven't smelled before, or a sudden strong bad smell.

To practice this, ask people to make loud or strange sounds from unexpected directions while your eyes are closed. Try to be aware of in which direction your attention is heading in the moment. The point of this exercise is to be aware of the *attention* that you are paying unconsciously to unknown stimuli. The sounds or the directions themselves do not matter.

Next is automatic object identification attention. After your attention shifts unconsciously, it switches its goal to identifying the object. This happens immediately after automatic space-oriented attention, so practice the two attentions together, trying to be aware of both.

The third kind of attention is intentional space-oriented attention. Unlike automatic attention, in this kind, you deliberately direct your attention to an intended object. For example, you might pay attention to a flowerpot intentionally and while doing so, you are aware of and understand what intentionally directed attention is. You feel that something inside of yourself is being sent out.

The last kind of attention, intentional object identification attention, is also one you are aware of. Note that, for example, when you look around with the intention to check where the flowerpot is, you are aware that first, your attention goes in a certain direction, and then, *the intention to identify* occurs.

The next practice is to determine what kind of attention you are using at any given time. Look around and choose 10 objects and keep them in your mind. Recall the first object and resolve yourself to check it in your mind before actually sending your attention toward it. Do the same with the other objects. While you are doing so, be aware of your attention, making sure to categorize it into the four kinds. The purpose of this exercise is to understand internally what using intentional space-oriented attention and intentional object identification attention is, and to realize that you can do it freely.

As you can see, we can differentiate our attention into various kinds. Differentiation, in its own way, can be another type of confinement. However, compared to when we don't differentiate, it is advantageous for us in that it helps our consciousness become sharper and our ability to be aware become deeper. If you start to carefully look into your attention while doing these exercises, you will gain the power to see *attention* itself as an object and gradually find that you can freely use intentional attention. As we begin to use attention intentionally, we gradually wake up from our so-called *sleep*. Sleep here means living your life unconsciously and automatically, swept away by the *happenings* of the world. Waking up from such sleep and pouring consciousness into what is present is present attention.

When I was little, I would visit my cousins in the countryside. I saw my uncle go to check on the rice fields early in the morning. When the fields needed more water, he would draw water into the rice field. This is what the Chinese character 注 in 注意 (attention) means: to draw water and pour it into something. It represents the meaning of the word attention, which is to pour one's will, consciousness, and life force into something, just as my uncle poured water into the rice field.

Once you can see each pattern of attention and tell its type, it is time to look at the depth of your attention. Each kind of attention is different in its level of depth. Let's try being aware of the level of your attention on an object. It is of course recommended that you only do this exercise after you can clearly determine the four *types of attention*. The purpose of this exercise is to see that the intensities of each kind of attention that you use are all different. First, prepare a paper, a pen, and a flowerpot or other object. Draw a horizontal line on the paper, divide the line into 10 equal parts, writing a number from one to ten on each of them. Second, send your attention weakly, as weak as you can, to an object around you, feel the intensity, and label it one. Then, send your attention strongly, as strong as you can, and call it 10. Muse over the attention levels one and 10, find a middle point, and set it as five. Now focus on the attention levels between one and five and between five to 10 and define them internally, like a sliding scale. When you are done defining the internal intensity of your attention in each scale, look at the flowerpot. Look at the top of the plant and pay level-one attention. Look slightly below and pay raise the level of your attention to level two. Continue until you reach the bottom of the flowerpot, by which point your attention level should be 10. All the while, notice how the intensity level of your attention changes.

As you practice these attention exercises, you will understand what it means to be *present*. Many people say to live in the moment and claim to be here and now. But, as you know well, just because you've heard and understood this in your head doesn't mean that you're really present. We are always surrounded by the past. Take a quick look around you right now. Is there anything that you don't think or feel you *know*? If you feel that you *know* all the things around you, it means that you are surrounded by *the past*, because all knowing is history. Therefore, *freedom from knowing* is freedom from the past, and freedom from all knowing means simultaneous death and rebirth.

Do you understand? It's a kind of *death*. Taking off the veil of knowing means nullifying your entire past and resetting it. This means rebirth because you enter the same state as when you were born, and also means that you have passed death to be reborn.

As newborn babies, we experience no knowing—everything is new and mysterious. But as we grow up, we build up more and more knowledge through learning and experience, to the point that when we are around 20 years old, we feel we have almost nothing more to know about the world. However, the truth is that we are trapped in the restricted confines of knowing rather than having nothing more unknown. In fact, the thought or the feeling of knowing is a shackle that makes a man a lonely *fragment* of existence. Albert Einstein, who deeply explored this physical world and learned more than anyone else, talked about the mysteries of the universe. Wittgenstein, who dug deeper into the world of logic than any other human, affirmed that "What we cannot speak about, we must pass over in silence." They both experienced the mystery beyond knowledge. They saw that no matter how much they knew, it was limited to Earth, that there were larger solar systems, galaxies, and countless vast super galaxies, and even beyond that there was an endless depth that could not be reached no matter how deeply they explored human reason.

They *experienced* this mystery but could not *exist* as the mystery itself. Only when you free yourself from the confines of knowing can you live as a nondual being that is truly whole with no separation.

Ironically, we can't see things as they are because we are covered with the hidden veil of knowing. Because of the feeling or thought of *knowing*, we ironically *don't know* the truth of being. So how can we be *present*? Being present in the moment is being in the state of not knowing. This is different from the *feeling* of not knowing. One doesn't feel familiar or acquainted when one is in the state of not knowing—one simply exists in the moment. Therefore, neither how many books you read nor how much you know has any effect on being able to experience the state of being present.

But when you practice this book's attention exercises, you will become more and more present. Becoming more present means that more of your life force is poured into any given moment. Because *attention* has no conscious *content*, it is impossible for it to contain *the past*, so it gradually returns to the present. The past is a tangible *thing*, like *a story*. But attention is not anything that you can name—it is a transparent life force. It is you shifting your center of existence toward the force. The closer you get to the force, the more you become present. Thus, you must begin with the practice of pouring your life force into *transparent attention without an object*. Feel your attention, be aware of the direction in which it moves, and measure the intensity of it in detail. Your attention in itself is a fruitful area for inquiry. Attention is the material of consciousness and the closest friend to your life force. It has almost no shadow. All our *knowledge* is a shadow. We can be one with a pine tree, but we cannot *know* the pine tree. Knowing is only a shadow of a pine tree and it is not the pine tree itself. We live in many shadows. Now it is time to come out of the world of shadows and meet the pine tree just as it is.

EXERCISE 1.2

Now we are going to do an application exercise. Look at the flowerpot again. Find the part of the flowerpot that attracts your attention the most. Observe it in detail and try to figure out why you are attracted to that particular part. For example, you might think, "I am attracted to the newly blooming leaf at the top. I'm attracted to the delicate, soft appearance of the leaf, and I'm also attracted to its straight vein..." and so on. While watching it, if you start to get attracted to another part, you can move your eyes to that. But you should be *conscious* of the attraction that you feel and consciously keep it in mind before you move your attention to a different part of the plant. For example, if, when you are observing the top of the plant, you sense your attention attracted down to a leaf below, this might be because you have spent enough attention at the top of the plant. At first, your eyes will want to move unconsciously (automatic space-oriented attention). However, resist the pull of automatic attention and only allow yourself to move your eyes after you tell yourself consciously, "My attention has been attracted to the lower left leaf." This is intentional space-oriented attention. If you happen to unconsciously move your attention, go back to the previous object and try to move consciously again. Always make sure you are aware of your attention before you move your eyes. In other words, always move your attention purposefully.

Next, let's try an exercise to check the quality of your attention. Again, observe a part of the plant that attracts you. Observe it carefully, making sure you understand why you are attracted to the part. For example, think, "I'm attracted to the dark blue leaf. I'm attracted to the strongly stretched vein of the leaf. I'm attracted to the leaf's strong vein." At the same time, be aware what level of your attention is being paid on a scale of one to 10. For example, "My attention to the dark blue color of the leaf is six. And as I pay more attention to the strongly stretched vein, it's an eight," and so on. Finally, look at the whole plant and gauge your overall level of attention.

Water Sees Not the Moon but Its Reflection

In this section, let us continue using the more comprehensive terms attraction and repulsion instead of "greed that desires" and "hatred that resists." The universal nature of the two concepts can be applied to individual humans' subconsciousnesses, the deeper collective subconsciousness, and also to the organic biosphere consciousness, so it is important to differentiate. There is always reason for attraction and repulsion. Looking deeply into the two, we find that they are directly connected to survival, or, when sublimated, associated with the movement to annihilate and merge into a whole. But we are not here to dig into them and reveal their cause. We just want to discover the truth about how *attention* moves, because the movement of attention is a phenomenon essential to understanding the conscious activity that causes the feeling of knowing. Only when we understand and experience attention can we recognize the *background* against which all experiences happen. However, the transition is very difficult. How is it possible to *know* the background of our consciousness when it is the source of our consciousness? It is difficult, but there is certainly a way.

The key is to notice the source of your attention rather than the cause of your attention. In order to do so, first focus on the difference in how your consciousness is attracted to and repulsed by an object. Paying attention to this difference will shift your center to the background and allow you to focus on the phenomena of attraction and repulsion.

This exercise will begin by sending attention to an object, just like before. This time, however, you will gradually notice that your attention to the object is actually being paid to your own *gamji* (image, sensation), which are what you use to identify the object, and in the end you will realize that you are only observing yourself. When you see yourself, move your focus away from your *gamji*, the images from the past, to the root of consciousness, which makes those images possible, then the seer and the seen will disappear.

When you are looking at an object for a long time and it becomes dull, you are using *gamji*. Only by using *gamgak* can you see the object as it is. Noticing that you are looking through *gamji* is like water thinking that it is looking at the moon before realizing that it is only seeing the reflection of the moon on its own surface. In the same way, it is not that we see things as they truly are but that we see their shadow being reflected off of our consciousness. We can never truly see or know the moon. We can only use *gamgak* on the moon. Thus, what we see is not the true nature of a thing but images of it reflected within us. These images are a part of our internal sensory information network that connects to all other things. As we move our attention to the water from the reflection of the moon, we can move our attention to the source of consciousness that enables an image, not to the inner image itself, when we look at things. All these practices are necessary to realize that the object of your attention is the reflection of the moon, not the moon itself, so you can move your attention to the water. Then, you will notice that the one who sees, the object that is seen, and the act of seeing are all functions of the water, and that the water is the source.

All existing beings push and pull each other. The universe aims for ceaseless movement through this, for movement is the first requisite for being proven alive. A moving thing draws more attention that a static thing. That is why constant movement—and the actions of push and pull—happens inside of us. There are no inside and outside in the universe. It is just one.

Most of our pain comes from this mental push and pull. Interestingly, however, attraction and repulsion are the result of the feelings or thoughts that have already accumulated within you or those that are being made right now. That is the standard that you are identified with. However, what we identify with is difficult for us to see because we are constantly in the state of identifying with our inner standard, instead. As we saw earlier in the process of consciousness arising, all objects appears along with the *I*. In other words, if you are attracted to an object, it means that you already possess something that is attracted to it and you identify with it. For example, if you are attracted to the south magnetic pole, that means you contain something of the north magnetic pole. In another example, you might ask, "Why am *I* only attracted to gentle people?" This is because you believe yourself to have something of a rough characteristic, so you are attracted to the inner qualities of an opponent who maintains tenderness in this harsh world. Another *I* could push way or resist a gentle and weak person. This is because this *I* has a weak side and, thinking that it is always losing, always tries to be tough and strong.

So, if you feel attraction or repulsion to a thing or a being that you consider external to yourself, this always means that you possess something identified as *I* that corresponds to the object. If you cannot find it, you will not be able to understand why you feel pain and anger. This is why it is often said that pain is born by unconscious resistance. In Buddhism, it is said that suffering is caused by the three poisons: greed, hatred, and ignorance. Greed is to be attracted to something, hatred is to refuse and push away, and ignorance is to not be aware of the coming and going of greed and hatred. Wisdom, on the other hand, is to see greed and hatred appearing and disappearing from the point of view of the whole and to notice that they always arise and disappear paired with *I*, as what I will call an "I-object."

Therefore, we can become free from *I* by *seeing* through all these identification that is the hidden and unseen *I*. To do this, you first have to learn to feel and discern mental attraction and repulsion and find their causes.

EXERCISE 2

First, look at the things around you and sense how much they resonate or don't resonate with your consciousness. At first, you may not be able to sense this. Look back and forth between a familiar object and an unfamiliar object, marking the difference in your attraction to them on the scale from one to 10. Once you can do this well, start thinking of people you've known for the past year one by one and see if you feel being attracted to them or pushing them away. Since we've divided the intensity of attention on a scale from one to 10, it would be good if you tried to measure the intensity of this push or pull on a scale from one to 10, too.

Anything that you are attracted to or push away is a mental *object*. The reason that you are attracted to or push away a mental object is because part of your *I* already identifies with it. If you can identify what part of the *I* causes your attraction or repulsion to the object, you can *drop* it right away. By doing so, you leap directly into *taiji* (literally "great pole") consciousness, or pure consciousness that extends beyond your inner world that is divided between you and I, subject and object, and yin and yang.

In other words, in order to return to pure consciousness, you must first see that your inner world is divided into "you and I," or "subject and object." Seeing *something* external to you is just evidence that you are already internally divided, for there is an *I* that sees something. In fact, *no-thing* exists outside of ourselves. It is just that we draw lines and discriminate by using *gamji*. The world is *seen* as the world simply because of our consciousness. Nothing *exists* that is divided. Therefore, if you are looking at something, you should be aware that you, the subject who sees the *world*, are divided at that very moment. Seeing something, *knowing* something, *feeling* something all mean that your mind is divided into "I and object." If this is the case, then, when is it that the inner world is not divided? It is when you are overwhelmed in front of a magnificent waterfall, or when you are no longer aware of yourself in front of an endless sea, only the sense of infinity remains. No feeling of *me* is there. There is no thought, no feeling, but only the sense of being present.

Fill It Up with Silence

Our inner world is always filled with silence. Silence is its default state. But when noise draws attention, movement forms and flows, creating circulation. Just as water turns into vapor and forms clouds, which produce raindrops that seep into the earth, pool together, and become vapor again, our attention gathers into thoughts, which accumulate into a mass that eventually becomes heavy and falls as a rain of emotion, seeps into existence, dissolves and disperses, and regains attention again. All of these are the universe's movements of internal and external circulation. Therefore, you can't experience silence by following your attention. You have to focus on the background of where the attention is taking place.

Why, then, are we unable to escape from the clamor of thought and emotion? Why do we not see thoughts or feelings? Modern science can create an invisible man. A person in a special garment of electrical conductors and optical sensors can project the image of what is behind him onto his body, making it appear transparent. It is not that light goes through his body, but that light information gathered by the optical sensor on the back of the apparatus is projected through the optical sensor on the front, making it appear as if light has penetrated his body.

Thus, being transparent means becoming one with one's

Picture 1

Picture 2

Picture 3

(Picture 1) Person wearing an outfit that has small sensors all over the front and back, like scales.
(Picture 2) The image from the sensors on the back is transmitted to the sensors on the front and begins to appear.
(Picture 3) As the background is shown on the sensors on the front, a person observing from the front may mistakenly think that the person has disappeared.

background; actual transparency is not achieved. This also happens in our consciousness. What this means is that if our thoughts or emotions identify with the source and are used as the basis for seeing and interpreting other people's thoughts or emotions, they become *invisible* to us. This is because we use our thoughts and emotions as a basis, and we call this phenomenon identification. However, identifying them is like looking at the background as shown in the picture above, confused. Therefore, by escaping the deceptive background to experience the true background of silence, you will finally be free from the noise of your feelings and thoughts.

There is a still and silent emptiness at the heart of each movement, quietly watching. Upon reading this, you might try to *see* the background of the silence. But you cannot see it because the background cannot be an object. Therefore, when a noise arises, you need to *become the silence* and look at the noise instead of trying to see the silence. Additionally, you need to notice that the reason why you can see the noise is because your very essence is silence.

EXERCISE 3

In this silence exercise, we will feel what silence is, become silence itself, and understand that **such an intrinsic silence feels *me*.** In order to do so, follow the steps below.

Look at a plant near you. Feel its wordless silence. Bring the silence to your heart and feel it there. Fill your body with the silence. Fill the entire room with the silence. Fill the entire space around you with the silence. While doing so, notice that the silence is not broken even if you hear a sound. When the sky, the earth, and the whole universe are filled with silence, you will have a glimpse of utmost happiness. Fill yourself with the feeling of euphoria. Fill the whole universe with the feeling. Realize that the silence is pure consciousness, of which the universe is full.

You should be careful not to do this whole process with an *image*. Make sure that you carry it out with a *feeling*, not an image in your mind. You must do it with the sensations that your body feels in the moment. Images happen in your mind and involve both the past and the future, but a feeling, at least, happens in the moment. So, it is more accurate to use feeling.

When you are filled with the feeling of silence, next feel the sounds inside you. Feel the sounds while you *existing as silence*. Notice that you cannot feel your true silence, only recognizing indirectly that you are the *silence* by registering the *sound*.

Absolute consciousness is not something that is far and unreachable. Absolute consciousness is always present, along with the relative consciousness that your everyday thoughts spread. It's like *taiji*, which always contains yin and yang. When the relative world of yin and yang stops, that's the world of *taiji*. When the troubled thoughts and feelings from which you suffer from stop, that is the absolute world. The relative world, with all its drama and stories, where *I* and *object* and this and that exist, is happening right on top of the absolute world at this very moment. They exist in the same spacetime, just like waves and water.

GAMJI

Who wakes up?

It is not me that wakes up.
It is an awakening from everything, including the *me*.

What Are *Gamji?*

The word *feeling* contains many different meanings. First and most basic is that of feeling tactile sensation. You can feel the surface of this book by touching it. You inevitably feel something. Let's go look at the surface levels of feeling first and gradually move on to the more fundamental ones.

The most superficial feelings are smooth, cool and pleasant, soft and warm, and so on. These are uncertain feelings expressed in words.

When you go one step down, there are even smaller feelings that precede words. In other words, something cool or soft still feels the same even when you touch it in slightly different ways, but the subtler feelings beyond words do change. These are difficult to express in words but there is a slight difference to them.

Going down one more step, there are sensory feelings that are not associated with feelings of knowing or thinking. These are indeed just feeling a thing as it is, with no thought or story interfering. Distorted images from one's past experience have no effect on these feelings. They are the feelings we had when we were born and started using our senses for the first time.

But this also sets the reaction between things and our senses as the inner standard. Going one step further, there is a conscious feeling. Actually, it would be better to call it conscious discrimination rather than feeling, as this is what distinguishes this from that, no matter how fine the difference is. But since the subtle difference is felt, it can still be called conscious feeling.

In this way, the action of feeling connects us to things in various dimensions.

When it comes to feeling, there is feeling through the five senses, and feeling through consciousness such as emotions, thoughts, and the subtle sense of existence. If you look at these as being on levels, emotions are on the surface, thoughts are below emotions, *gamji* are below thoughts, even deeper are pure *gamgak*, and the source is the deepest level.

Now, put down your book for a moment and go out and feel the things and creatures that you find outside. At first, you will immediately enter the dimension of emotions, or the dimension in which emotions and thoughts are mixed. Or you will enter the dimension of *gamji* (memory), which can be considered boredom, since everything out there is known to you. Typically, we either just pass by things thinking that we know them already or end up staring at one thing out of an expectation that it might contain something that we don't know. But instead of focusing on everything new that comes into your awareness, pay attention to what passes too quickly for you to grasp. Because we immediately identify with the thoughts or emotions that arise every time we see something, we overlook the essential basic steps that come before them. Therefore, it's important to harbor an interest in what happens just before a thought or emotion happens.

From the source to the surface, our consciousness is a single body, but each level is separate and works differently, like the ocean. The surface is constantly choppy with waves, but at the same time the depths are still, silent, and secretly humming.

According to classical physics, what we see is photons bouncing off of external objects and entering our eyes, stimulating cone and rod cells there to result in vision. From this technical perspective, seeing is clearly a passive activity. However, the phenomenon of seeing is not so simple. If responding to stimuli is seeing, then we would be no different than a litmus paper whose color changes when exposed to chemicals. Our visual cells would be simply responding to stimuli. What, from this simple response, then leads to the experience of seeing something? In this sense, the cause of seeing has still not been discovered scientifically.

Here's a new scientific hypothesis. I propose it because I think it will be helpful in explaining *gamji* in relation to this book's exercises. As Susan Greenfield and Rodolfo Llinás say, seeing is a kind of mental projection, which supports the definition of *gamji*.

Rodolfo Llinás, a professor in the Department of Physiology & Neuroscience at the NYU Grossman School of Medicine, says in the BBC documentary series *Brain Story* (episode 3, "Mind's Eye"), that seeing is just another form of dreaming:

> If you consider what happens when you dream, you find that, amazingly, you actually do feel pain and you do feel surprised— you see things, you hear things, and people that you know talk

to you in a proper language with proper intonation. So what that tells you is that dreaming and being awake are next of kin, if not exactly the same thing. And if this is the case and this is the hypothesis, then we will begin to really understand what the brain is about because the brain is about making images. Basically, the brain is a dreaming machine. It is the brain that generates reality. It creates reality, so to speak. The reality is modulated. It's limited by the senses. We need to see. We need to perceive. We need to dream actively because this is the only way that we can take this huge universe and put it inside very tiny head. We fold it. We make an image and we project it out. That's what we do.

He argues that images created in our brain are converted into *facts* using external information. In other words, that we *recognize* something as a rock, tree, or computer is the result of us *developing* our internal images by referring to external information. Through this development, we perceive whatever we see as *factual*. Of course, it is controversial to say that this is all within our brains, but there is good reason to focus on Llinás's point that *seeing* is a system of *development* that we are accustomed to.

Susan Greenfield, in the same documentary, says, "Vision is not about simply soaking up the outside world. Instead, it's an active process which invents, ignores, and distorts what's entering through the eyes.... It's not so much that our visual system rebuilds the outside world. Rather, we create from scratch our own private universe, our own reality" (Brain Story episode 3, "Mind's Eye").

Greenfield and Llinás mention that the act of seeing is not simply the input of external information, but the identification and projection of it using internal information. This contains the same idea as in the phrases "A man sees only what he wants to see" or "The world is an illusion" because it means that the world looks different depending on how we see it—the eye of the *viewer* always affects *what he sees*.

We use the term *gamji* in this book. *Gamgak* and *gamji* are similar but different. When you look at the relationship between increase of brain capacity and age, you can see that the increase is extremely rapid—nearly a vertical line on a graph—until one reaches three years old, at which point the line flattens. This means we absorb information and learn the most until age three.

Until age three, we use *gamgak* while learning. Then, we gradually start to use *gamji* as we develop our own network of information. To use *gamgak* is to feel through the five physical senses, and to use *gamji* is to feel through the recollection of traces of *gamgak*. Therefore, to use *gamji* is to see something as it is

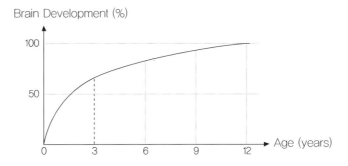

reconstructed by our mind, not *as it actually is*. *Gamji* means to feel (*gam*) and to know (*ji*) while *gamgak* mean to feel (*gam*) and to realize right at the moment (*gak*). When we say "I know," we mean that we have compared what we are experiencing with what we have inside. You can say that you *know* only when you have traces of the *past* accumulated inside of yourself. A child who sees a tree for the first time in his life is busy using *gamgak* to see the tree. He absorbs and feels everything around him. There is nothing he uses *gamji* for. He sees without having any feeling of knowing. But most people over twenty now use *gamji*. Over 90 percent of what they see, they see with a feeling of knowing or of at least partial recognition. At this age, thoughts and images begin to rule one's life. One dances on the guitar strings of such emotions as pain, misunderstanding, shame, and pride.

It is at this moment that our life needs a leap. This is because we feel frustrated deep inside at the way that we experience everything through a single *frame*, restricted by the way we see the world through a sense of knowing. This is called *self*. Of course, without it, we would *know* nothing of the *world*. But sooner or later we have to go beyond knowing. With this comes *freedom*. Freedom comes only when we can distinguish our senses of *gamji* and *gamgak* when we look at something and remain separate from them.

To apply Rodolfo Llinás's words to our practice, images created in the brain and projected outwards are *gamji*, and external information that we take makes up *gamgak*. When these two meet and are compared with each other, a feeling of *knowing* occurs.

And the phenomenon of being *conscious* happens when there is any change, no matter how big or small, in the feeling of knowing which constantly comes and goes.

For more about *gamji*, you can refer to the Being Awake Testimonials titled "Catching the Moment a Thought Arises" on page 237.

EXERCISE 4

Now, before we start our full-scale *gamji* exercises, we must practice discovering them first. You can practice by following the steps below.

1) Look at the things around you and try to feel them in two ways: first, by calling their names and second, without calling their names. Note the changes in how you feel their presence. Can you tell the difference between how you feel an object when you call its name and how you feel an object when you don't? Aside from the name of a thing and thoughts related to the name, the simple *familiar feeling* and the feeling that you don't know something's name are the result of *gamji*. Practice on many things around you.

2) Think of your parents or siblings and feel them by calling their names, or titles such as "mother," "father," or "brother." Then get rid of the names and watch for changes in your inner feelings.

Unconscious *gamgak* build up unconscious *gamji*. When unconscious *gamji*, which are the inner accumulation of one's past, meet with the *gamgak* that come in from the outside, attraction and repulsion within the *gamji* occur, and attention (life energy) moves and generates thoughts. These thoughts lead to attraction and repulsion again, and emotions arise and action begins through identification with the attraction and repulsion.

We all have to start somewhere, so we cannot help but to start from *ignorance*. In the state of ignorance, a network is formed by the accumulation of feelings by using *gamgak*. And the tendency, that is, the energy pattern formed through this network, is a vector that moves in a certain direction.

What is a vector? It's a movement. And movement always needs direction. Our minds, too, are always on the move, otherwise they cannot exist. The mind is a collection of memories, an interdependent network. So when you pay attention to one memory, it brings you to another memory, and this reaction triggers another, over and over. It is in the mind that memories are constantly aroused and running toward each other. In other words, memory depends on other memories. One vector depends on another. What if a vector, a force with direction, loses its direction? It stops where it is, an aimless force. This phenomenon is like seeing a cosmos flower swaying in the wind. At first, your attention, your life force, is drawn to it by its shaking, its color, and its swaying stem. And when you reach the flower, your eyes fix upon its marvelous gradations and delicacy. You immerse yourself into its beauty, resulting that the viewer disappears and only the beauty of the flowers exists. At that moment, the vector of consciousness that moves your *I* toward the *flower* disappears. Now you can escape of memory and see the flower as it is.

So, what is it like to escape memory? We consider *gamji* to be all memories, from the minuscule to the obvious. This is because they bring about feelings of familiarity and knowing.

The first step is to check your *gamji* using sound. Let's listen for sound coming from outside right now. If you listen carefully, you can distinguish between the *sound* itself, the *concept of sound*, and your *reaction to the sound*. For example, if you hear a car around, try to distinguish the s*ound* of the car itself, the *concept* of the sound of a car, and your *reaction* to the sound, such as one of enjoyment or displeasure.

When you can distinguish the three, the next step is to focus attention and fix focus on the *sound itself*. To focus attention is to spend about 10 seconds focusing on the sound itself, and to fix focus is to spend about 120 seconds (two minutes) on it. In the beginning, it may be difficult to concentrate and fix your attention to the sound itself. So first, try to focus and fix your attention to the *concept of the sound (a car sound)*. While doing so, you may be able to identify the *sound itself*, instead of *a car sound*. In other words, when your attention is focused on a car sound itself, you will be taken a step further and be immersed in the sound itself, leading to the state of fixed attention, in which your flow of consciousness is not broken. Then, you can experience the concept of a *car* dropping out of the *sound of a car* so that only a *sound* is heard. As the state continues, in which you are concentrated on the *sound itself*—the nature of the object—and hear the *sound* without it being distorted by the feeling or image of a *car*, this is called *non-gamji focus*. This is a highly state of strong concentration that is not distorted by *gamji*.

The unknown values of X and Y exist like reeds that depend on each other, as do the feeling of *I* and the feeling of *object*. Reeds can never stand alone. They can only stand by supporting each other. Likewise, the feelings of *object* and *I* can exist only if they rely on each other, and what arises from this relationship is consciousness. That is, the feeling of knowing arises when *object* and *I* meet. In this way, *object*, *I*, and *knowing* are three friends who are always together. Therefore, when you set aside the feeling of knowing and start looking at things, the *things* that you'd previously known disappear and things start to look unfamiliar to you. This state of unfamiliarity expands until all that is left is *unknown*. This state of unknown is the state of *gamgak*. By this point, the feeling of *I* also disappears, because a subject and an object and the feeling of knowing that allows the two to relate to each other come and go altogether. To reach this point, remove the name from an object that your *I* see, remove its shape and its quality. Then, the object will gradually disappear and only *seeing* will remain.

Feeling Neutral

When you practice *gamji* exercises, sometimes emotions occur that stop you in your tracks. This means that you have actually already been swayed by the relative world, with some internal sense of being pushed by or pulled to the *gamji*. As long as you do not blindly follow what you are attracted to nor push away what repulses you, and try to feel those feelings neutrally, you will gradually gain back the strength to practice. Once you're aware of your attraction and the repulsion, you'll come to know what a neutral state is, without being drawn in or pushing away. Once you are familiar with it, pay attention to that neutral state.

Attraction and repulsion are deeply related to our emotions. Attraction and repulsion are measured as follows:

+5	+4	+3	+2	0	−2	−3	−4
Strong Attraction				Neutral			Strong Repulsion
Eagerness	Exultation	Attachment	Fun	0 (Zero)	Sadness	Dislike	Anger
慾	喜	愛	樂		哀	惡	怒

As shown in this table, attraction feels good and repulsion feels bad. Therefore, the fact that there are good feelings and bad feelings means that there is a hidden standard within *me*, by which *I* would be attracted to or repulsed encountering an object, and on which the energy is centered. In other words, our emotions are not pure sensory feelings, but secondary feelings, reinterpretations and reconstructions of our attraction and repulsion.

A hot-blooded person is a someone who has a lot of energy. This kind of person's experience of these secondary feelings exhibits a strong polarity. Only when he escapes this polarity will he be able to make a good use of his abundance of energy. When the neutral energy deviating from this polarity feels and identifies with attraction or repulsion, an energy channel is formed and the energy shows as a strong emotion. Energy, vitality, prana, and qi are neutral energies that we can use, and major emotions, which are unconsciously taught in human society, act as passages for energy to vent. However, in order for these passages to work, inner identification must happen first. What we're going to do is use *gamgak* on the feelings of *attraction* and *repulsion* that occur before inner identification happens so we can be *awake* to those feelings.

When you are able to control being awake at any time, you won't have to stop the identification that happens within you. The major emotions are a tool to use just like a keyboard. We use keyboards to communicate with computers, just as humans use emotions to communicate with other humans. If you can freely use your emotions as a tool of communication, you should do so. Restraining is not a good use of our hard-earned tools. However, we should not depend too heavily on our tools, either. The guiding determinant to tell if you use them at your will is to ask *whether you can stop any given emotion at any given time.* If you can stop at any time, then you have full control over your use of emotions. But if you can't stop, then you yourself are being *used* by the emotions, having fallen into them.

When you feel confused, don't feel like practicing anymore, and want to quit, do this *Feeling Neutral* exercise. While feeling repulsion, try to recall the opposite feeling, thinking about a time that you were attracted to something. And as you swing between attraction and repulsion, gradually find a middle point where you are neither drawn nor push away anymore.

If you get a headache or feel pained, drowsy, or numb in this process, ask yourself, "What does consciousness look like in this state? How does the pain I feel in my head affect the quality of consciousness itself?" It is at this point that you will feel the quality of consciousness remain unchanged. Then, ask again: "Where is this headache? It doesn't affect the quality of my consciousness, so who and what is it affecting?" Ask yourself and examine what effect the pain has.

Attraction and repulsion happen all the time. They are life-sustaining actions. However, it is problematic to be identified with them and pour life energy into them, instead of just seeing them as signals. In other words, emotions always rise and disappear. You don't have to actively get rid of them. This means we can control how we feed into them, and how they feed on us. If you identify yourself with your emotions, you create a pathway to them, constantly supply energy to them, and feed them. Every energy channel occurs through identifying. So, if you could simply observe emotions arising and stop identifying yourself with emotions as they arise, they simply become useful messengers that we can use as a guide to survival and a better quality of life. This is using emotions well. One will be angry, happy, afraid, and sad when necessary. But one will not fall into these emotions.

Now, what does "fall into" mean?

Every emotion has a deep meaning and is a useful tool for life. Let's take a closer look at this through the emotion of *fear*. Fear has something to do with the future. We feel anxious that what's going to happen will not go the way we want it to. We feel worried and concerned about what's to come. Fear is a kind of *signal* that causes us to have worry (negative) and concern (positive). Worry (苦悶) means distress (苦) and nervousness (悶). This destroys your body and mind. But concern (念慮) is to think (念) about how to resolve the fear and consider (慮) an attitude with which to cope with it. The ideation that the future is going to be troublesome and difficult signals itself through a moment of *fear*. The reason we hold onto this signal and worsen our own distress is that we only *worry* about it. If you turn to *concern* instead of worrying, fear will disappear after a while. Turning to concern means your energy will be used for a solution. And the signal of fear, triggered by small signs from the present, can be a useful aid in solving future problems smoothly. Consider that without fear you might not have taken action to seek a solution to a problem. Therefore, fear is a powerful preparation device for anyone who is awake enough to use it.

The reason why we fall into fear instead of using it is because we only worry, digging up past data from our accumulated *gamji* and inflating it into distorted imaginations. At this moment, you are pouring all your energy into distress and anxiety, and you can't get out of there. At this moment, do the *Feeling Neutral* exercise. Recall the feelings of attraction and repulsion that you have experienced in the past, and then move back and forth between them, feeling for a neutral zone in between. This is like being at "zero" on the emotional level scale. Staying in this zone will free you from emotional confusion.

Feeling the Foundation of the Sense of Separation

Every object or particle has its own boundary. Everything that I can feel or be conscious of has individual boundaries. Without individual boundaries, we cannot perceive things, because if we can't distinguish between this and that, we can't know them as two separate things. The same goes for everything we can sense or know, from inanimate things to plants, animals, people, and even feelings, thoughts, and presences. A spatial or temporal gap must define something from the things around it for it to be identified as an individual. When you clearly understand the boundaries of all external and inner beings, you will notice many things that were not previously understood.

To know is to build boundaries. Every individual with boundaries can be considered a particle, and each also has wave nature or totality, so in individuality they are separated and bounded at the same time. We call it the basis. All our conscious phenomena are bounded by their particle nature, and also have unseparated wave nature. That wave nature is the basis.

Consciousness always flows in search of newness—that its very nature. Newness always has unchangeability at its very core. It is like how we find ourselves still though we are moving, such as in a vehicle. We are simultaneously constantly changing sound and endlessly motionless silence. If you feel you're in sound, you exist as a wave; if you feel you're in silence, you exist as water. Since we are both sound and silent at the same time, we are both wave and water. But, for most of our lives, we live believing that we are just waves, separate from each other. Believing that we are a separate sound, we identify ourselves with it, therefore live in the world of a separate you and a separate I.

The same goes for thoughts. The strong, colorful stimuli of thoughts and emotions are more attractive than pure consciousness, which is plain and clear, like water. And just like with all other sensory stimuli, we get desensitized. We crave stronger and stronger stimulation. So, we seek stronger thoughts and emotions. Right now, look inside yourself and find pure consciousness. Pay attention to the thoughts and feelings that accompany it. As with food, when you become accustomed to a strong flavor, you will grow distasteful of light and plain foods even when they are the most basic and commonly eaten food in your daily life. Likewise, our consciousness becomes more and more accustomed to highly stimulating thoughts and emotions, which leads to our energy no longer being direct to consciousness, which is so tasteless and transparent that it gets forgotten. We forget that it is that consciousness that can sustain us for a long time, like a simple daily meal or a staple food. In pure consciousness, thoughts and feelings can show various characteristics.

Choose two objects near you. Objects within a meter are fine. Focus your eyes on the empty space between the two, and make your mind conscious of both things. In other words, your eyes might see an empty space, but your consciousness remains placed on the two things. At some point, your consciousness will move away from the two objects and drift into the consciousness itself. At that moment, try to naturally move your attention to the consciousness itself and hold that state as long as possible. Focus on the consciousness for 12 seconds, fix your attention for two minutes, and perform non-*gamji* focus for 30 minutes. If this goes well, move on to the next exercise.

The Sea of Energy

When you wake up in the morning and feel thirsty, try to feel the rhythm of the universe in that thirst. Why does it always happen? As soon as you open your eyes, your thoughts bubble up and energy rushes to them. What force causes this? Feel the universal force that is present in everything. Thinking about and feeling the cosmic flow will thrill you. Why is that? It's frustrating to wake up in the same old room, and you'll likely feel like going out. Why is that you want change? What moves you to do such a thing? It is because your flow and the flow of the universe run together as one. Let's feel the flow.

Inside us, there is a wise being that is greater than who we think we are. This being always shares wisdom with us. But too often we are focused on our superficial selves and miss the being's subtle signals. Whenever we seek something, the signals come as wisdom, but they are so subtle and so instantaneous that we usually miss it. It's been a long time since we closed the door to those signals, and it's up to us to open the door. As long as you know how to open the door in the frame of *I* and exit through it, there is wisdom that you can access anytime, and you will meet the greatest wisdom in the universe. As long as you truly want it and are prepared...

This great wisdom flows inside of us like a huge storm. But

what on earth am *I* who cannot even notice or feel the presence of such a powerful storm? Put all your *gamji* down for a moment, put down all your images and thoughts, and wait with a seeking heart. Only a heart that seeks will guide the way. There is a great being who, if you believe in your own greatness, will not be troubled by any barrier or affected by the sorrow of any being at all.

There is a cosmic rhythm, an ocean of energy that binds the universe together. It is a matrix of energy that can flow through both the slight body of a child and the muscular body of a giant.

Do not think any thoughts, do not stir up any feelings—just wait with a longing heart for the ocean of the universe's energy, thinking of yourself as a drop of water that belongs to it. The ocean can come as an overwhelming fullness in your heart, as magnificent silence, or as thrilling bliss. But no matter the form in which it comes, you must seek it and attempt to become one with it.

As you read the above, did you feel any energy in your body? The sensation can be that of rocking energy, silence, or subtle joy. Close your eyes and amplify that feeling, closing all doors to outside sensations. Feel its enormity surround your body, surround the room you are in, and expand across the entire city, the entire country, and the entire planet. You will see that this feeling is not merely your imagination, that it was never the product of a powerless idea in your head, a single imagined thought. The feeling is alive and connected to the whole universe. Try it out. Experience it. Pour out your whole being to find this ocean of energy. There will come a certain moment when you feel an uninterrupted flowing. It will no longer feel like you are in control, and you will feel like you are disappearing in the flow of energy. This is not a result of ignorance; it is the phenomenon of self-abandonment that comes from entering an elevated state of consciousness. It is an explosion of pure energy, a feeling of tremendous freedom released from our infinite source that had been focusing on *I*.

It's like an explosion of energy in the middle of this ocean. The boundaries between substance, emotion, and thought, which are considered to be an apparent separate self, disappear, and inside and outside become one, revealing the ocean of energy is the only thing that exists. It's like one stream of water flowing through a huge ocean. Air flows through air, and water flows through water, and energy flows through energy.

EXERCISE 7

Once you have experienced the energy flow a little bit, lightly touch the back of your left hand with the fingers of your right hand, as if you were touching your first love's hand, as if you were brushing someone who you're not supposed to touch. Concentrate on the feeling of the gentle touch. Do you feel that lightness?

Now, take that infinitely light feeling to your chest and fill your whole body with it. Let that lightness be your existence. Slowly sway your body from side to side with the feeling. You can start with a very subtle movement first. Then, as the energy spreads all over your body, make the swaying bigger and bigger. The important thing is that the feeling on the unbearable lightness on the back of your hand goes to your heart and is conveyed back to your entire body. Practice this for 10 minutes.

This time, touch your palms together very gently, like a feather on closed eyelids. You will feel some joy. Do this for two minutes, then repeat for another two minutes. If you can continue without resting, do so. Just touch your palms together without pressing. The moment you press, take notice and adjust. Think about bringing the center of your existence to your awake consciousness. Don't focus on the soreness of your arms. Feel your body fall further into relaxation. And then touch your palms together again. Let the feather-like lightness enter your chest. Feel the feather-like lightness in your heart. And let that lightness be who you are.

The lightness can turn into weightlessness. What is featherlight can be blown away in a moment. Likewise, our feeling of *I am* is so light that it can disappear with just a single puff of air. The feeling that *I am* or *I exist* can disappear just like that. When that feeling disappears, there is nothing but an infinite weightless consciousness. From that moment, your consciousness will leap from the name, form, and qualities that you have identified with as *I* to a pure consciousness that is nameless, formless and qualityless.

The Pastness of *Gamji*: Memory

The old teachings said to stop changes and movement and revert to a quiet place, but now it is time, despite all the changes and movements, to realize the tranquility that has been here all along. This will be the trend of teaching in the future and a new teaching 2,500 years after Buddha. Those signs can be seen here and there, and their meanings are conveyed unconsciously through many of the consciousness development programs that have already begun to be deeply instilled in society. So far, it's not easy to deal with both movement and stillness at the same time, so they teach us to return to stillness first. But now it's time to manifest true stillness in movement and movement in stillness. Beyond the mechanism of memory, when we escape the feeling of *knowing*, we see that *not knowing* is at the source of ever-changing knowing, which is itself the movement in the stillness. In other words, we realize that movement is stillness.

All *knowing* is repetition of experience. To feel that you *know* is the result of subtle memories of past experiences that are brought back to experience again. When you can distinguish the feeling of *knowing* from what you feel when you encounter anything—objects, emotions, or thoughts, you can get to deal with *knowing*, i.e. memory. Then memory gradually falls away, and consciousness returns to the here and now, beginning to use *gamgak* on the present.

To do this, we first need to distinguish between *gamgak* and *gamji*, and we have clearly learned about *gamji* before. To put it simply again, to use *gamgak* is to feel (*gam* 感) and realize (*gak* 覺) present stimuli, and to use *gamji* is to feel (*gam* 感) and know (*ji* 知) by comparing to the past. Children mostly stay in feeling (*gam* 感) because they don't have much accumulated *gamji* to know (*ji* 知). So, children live the present. Adults, on the other hand, feel and go straight into knowledge; in other words, they go directly to the past. Therefore, it would be more correct to say that adults do not experience the present but re-experience the past with the present as a clue.

On the contrary, an enlightened person feels and realizes (*gak* 覺) what they are feeling (*gam* 感). They remove the sense of knowing from what they feel in daily life, which is *gak*. Memories, which are traces of experiences, are always accompanied by feelings of *I*, *it*, and *knowing*. To be exact, memories always wear a primary name tag that says *I* and a secondary name tag called *it*. So if you look at an object and take away all the memories related to its name, form, and quality, the *I* that you have identified as part of them disappears, and only *gam* and *gak* remain.

When you move from using *gamji* to using *gamgak*, you move from past to present, from *knowing* to simply realizing *as it is*. It is at this point that you will realize that all *knowing* wears name tags called *mine*, and *I*, *object*, and *knowing* are all one process.

It is the feeling of *I* that ties all disconnected thoughts together. For example, imagine you are watching raindrops falling. If the speed of your eyes watching them is slower than the speed at which they fall, they seem to be not individualized raindrops but long streaks of rain. In the same way, when fragments of memory and thought, which are traces of past individual experiences, arise and pass through the screen of pure consciousness, if the speed of your awareness of them is slower than their speed, you see them as a single continuous entity. This makes you mistake them for an apparent individual, which causes the feeling of *I*. When you look closely at your thoughts and see your consciousness become delicate, you can find the space between them and realize that the feeling of *I* labeled on each memory is actually separate fragments. Then you will see that the *I* was an entity, a fictitious name tag. In other words, all objects are different from one another, but because you cannot see them as separate raindrops, you mistake them for *I*, connecting them together like a sheet of rain.

Consciousness has an object, while awareness is awakened mind without objects. However, in this state, there can be moments of danger. The mind has the surprising ability to turn even the state of being awake without objects into a fixed trace, therefore objectifying this state. So if your awareness is not sensitive, even though you feel that you are in the state of being awake without objects, you may actually be in an objectified version of it. In other words, if there is a *knower* who says "I'm in pure consciousness," the feeling of *knowing* itself indicates an image composed of the past. If there's one criterion that distinguishes true from false awakenment, *being awake* is always *in progress*, not fixed. No matter how delicate it is, if it's an image, it's fixed. If you were drawing an image of something, you'll get sleepy or fall asleep.

That's because that the state of being awake is not alive, but dead. If you feel that the state that you are in is fixed, you are in an image—a memory. Being awake means *ceaseless, present-tense* existence. If you don't understand any of these words and feel like *you don't know*, you just need to be awake to the feeling of *not knowing*, since the feeling of not knowing is also a memory.

The process of being awake involves learning that everything, from big, coarse memories to small, delicate ones, is a memory and practicing releasing them. What this means is that you must realize that the feeling of knowing indicates that you are re-experiencing past memories. Everything is a memory. Every feeling that you know of is a memory. Even if it is pain, everything you are familiar with is a memory.

Freedom comes when you are liberated from all memories, which, of course, means everything you *know*. Additionally, once you *consciously* free yourself from a specific memory, it will pave the way for you to do the same with others.

There are various types of memory. When you feel a strong, vital force, this is the *memory of life force*. Going one step further, there is sexual memory. Sex here means bipolarity. One's life force has polarity and this causes an imbalanced state that inclines you toward being identified with either yin or yang. In this state, energy that you feel has a polarizing quality becomes sexual power through your *memory of bipolarity*. Next, there is *emotional memory*. This is the movement of energy stemming from the origin of two opposite qualities, where these opposite powers are attracted to and push away from each other, resulting in sensibility and emotion.

120

The *memory of love* is created by combining two opposite qualities through interaction. This love initially starts from a vital, physical force and gradually integrates with the universe of subtle energy to form the *memory of platonic love*. Then, the subtle movement of mind and intelligence occurs in earnest and there is the *memory that we call the conscious universe*. Finally, there is *spiritual memory* created by integrating these memories of intelligence and mind into one.

All of these processes are identical to the process of a baby being born and starting to use their life force. However, there is only one difference, which is that some people stop growing up at stage four, while other people grow up to stage seven. Memory consists of traces that are created in these various processes. The traces start from physical vital force and go through feelings created by interacting with life forces' two opposite qualities before finally being integrated in the delicate mind. These traces are largely classified as physical memory, emotional memory, and mental memory, but they also can be minutely classified as physical memory, sexual memory, emotional memory, the memory of love, the memory of platonic love, mental memory, and spiritual memory.

The fastest way to be liberated from memory is to start with thoughts. This is because, although the source of thought is definitely the life force, for human beings, the life force is coordinated by thought. This is similar to the fact that the source of energy is people, but a person who commands energy is a leader. Therefore, if you can deal with the leader, you can use the life force properly.

Can you abandon your thoughts? Can you let them go? If so, you can say that you are above your thoughts and experience them. In addition, you are liberated from mental memory. However, if you only are liberated from your thoughts when replacing them with other thoughts, you are not truly free. This is because you would not be able to do it if there were not other, more attractive thoughts tearing you away from your current ones.

I repeat again. Can you let go of your feelings? If so, that means that you are above your feelings and you are liberated from emotional memory. However, for instance, only if you can heal a broken heart by finding another lover, you are not truly free from feelings. You cannot let go of your current feelings without another to grab on to.

Can you let go of your sexual desires or cravings for food right now? If so, you liberated from physical memory. Nevertheless, for instance, if you cannot give up your appetite even though you are currently not hungry, you are tied up in your physical memory. In this case, it is necessary to distinguish physical *gamgak* which is a hunger for survival, from physical *gamji* which is a desire to eat.

Of course, it is okay that you enjoy the benefits of using your thoughts, emotions, sexual desires, and appetite. However, you must be able to freely let them go anytime. If you don't, you are just a robot who is tied to memory.

To gain this freedom, the most essential thing is to distinguish the memory piled up in your mind from *gamgak*—what you actually feel right now. How do you feel right now? Have you felt bored, nervous, empty, stifled, and refreshed before? If so, try to differentiate the familiar feeling of the past, and mark the boundary of that feeling, and feel it. The fact that you feel something means that it can be distinguished from others and being distinguishable means that there is a boundary. Examine for familiarity in every single feeling. These are all the past, memories, restored files, such as:

- Instinct memory: memories engraved in your genes, created by combining sensation, emotion, and an understanding of survival. (This memory will not be addressed because it is for survival. It will be addressed in an intensive course in another book.)
- Physical memory: *gamji* related to the five senses (different from reaction to sensation).
- Emotional memory: *gamji* related to emotional feelings that can be felt through the movement of inner energy.
- Understanding memory: *gamji* related to the feelings that arise when thought or intellectual understanding occurs.

These physical, emotional and understanding memories mostly manifest themselves at the same time. For instance, when it comes to an understanding about a scary situation, the energy moving along the overall context of understanding is emotion. In this way, energy (emotion) that moves in a particular structure (understanding) to affect the body is made up of physical *gamji*.

By the way, whatever you are feeling at this moment includes all three of these factors. These three factors always come together. However, since one of them always reveals itself as dominant, it is easy for you to feel only the dominant one.

For instance, when you feel uncomfortable due to a difference of opinion, the intensity of the feeling would be about level two, and among what you are feeling, emotional memory takes up 80 percent, followed by sensory memory and understanding memory at 10 percent each.

For example, think about two different situations in which someone might hold your arm. Even though you think of the same pressure, one might be what you imagine in order to explain what pressure is, and the other might be what you imagine when you think about an assailant holding your arm in a dark alleyway. There is a huge difference between these two feelings. In the case of the first one, sensory memory takes up the largest amount of the memory at play here, accounting for 80 percent, followed by understanding memory at 15 percent and emotional memory at five percent. In this case, the strength of the general feeling is about level three. However, in the case of the second one, the percentage of emotional memory (fear) was 90 percent, followed by sensory memory (the feeling of your arm being held) at seven percent, and understanding memory (grasping the situation) at three percent, with the strength of general feeling at about level nine. In this way, these three types of memory usually occur at the same time so you can deal with them as *one* feeling.

What is knowing? It is proof that there is a memory related to whatever stimuli you are taking in. Every single thing you see is a subtle memory. Therefore, knowing is the past. From now on, you should focus not only on paying attention to enlightened consciousness but also on remembering the fact that objects you're looking at right now are just old memories. In other words, feel things *the way that they are* and *the way that you remember them* at the same time.

EXERCISE 8

Earlier, we distinguished the *feeling of knowing* acquired by looking at an object and the past experience from the *feeling of something new* at the moment; then we let go the feeling of knowing and dived into the feeling sensed here and now. Now, let us look at various objects and separate an object's *gamgak* from its *gamji* and look at the two different results at the same time.

First of all, look at an object, pay attention to its boundaries, and try to see it *as it is*. By the way, even if you do not know what looking at something the way it is really feels like, just try, thinking about abandoning all your memories of the past. Now, pay attention to the object again and look at the *memory* of it. If you know what looking at the *memory* means, you are already free from the memory. You have escaped the past. The biggest problem is the fact that you don't know it when you are living in the past. As you get older, it is easier to stay in the past, recalling good old memories. When this happens, you do not actually realize that you are trapped in the past. In this state, when you look at an object in front of you, what you are seeing is the past. First, if you're looking at an object that you've seen at least once, it means you're definitely seeing the past. Second, If you're looking at an object that you would have probably seen before, it means you are seeing the object itself, plus part of the past. If you're looking at an object that you've never seen before, but feels like familiar somehow, it also means you're seeing the object itself plus the past. Therefore, separate the *memory* of the past from the object you are looking at now and then look at the remaining part. This is distinguishing between memory and a thing itself.

If you can differentiate between them well, next try to look at an object as *memory* and then *as it is* alternately. Try this with non-living things like rocks, first, and then try with plants, like flowers. If you can do this well, now try it by smelling instead of looking at the flowers. Scent also has an aspect of memory, but you can smell without memory. When this happens, the scent becomes one that you have never smelled before, and you can experience *the way that it is* beyond surface level.

For example, look at a ceiling light. Now, distinguish the feeling of 'this is what I know.' If a feeling continues, yesterday and today, it is a memory. Separate the memory out.

Look at an object and distinguish your memory of it from the way it is. Then, feel them simultaneously or one by one.

Move your attention back to the whole room and feel the silence around the object.

Move back to the object and feel the thing as *memory* and *the way it is* alternately.

Repeat this whole process five times. If you can go on, repeat until an insight occurs.

Finding the Center of Existence

Existence means being separated. Because in order for a person to exist, he has to be himself, not another person. This means that he has fallen out of the whole and is conscious of *being himself.* If he were not separated, he would not feel his own existence.

By the way, in the case of existence, there is more than one dimension. In other words, you do not exist as *someone*—there is just *being* in the dimension. This means that you exist not just as an individual but as *being*, the substance of all individuals, the essence of existence.

I cannot forget the beauty of the first field of poppy flowers I ever saw. At first, a single flower caught my eye and I was attracted to its petals. which were like red lights shining through very thin and soft sheet of *hanji* (Korean traditional paper). I was immediately fascinated by the ceremony of red and yellow flowers spreading across the whole field. Straight poppy stems swung gently in the wind and wide, soft flower petals spread out, stamens seeming to shine between them. Hundreds of thousands of flowers bloomed in the wide field. They rustled and danced in the breeze.

While I was watching them, fascinated by the scene, *I* was not there. Afterwards, when I went back home, I might have remembered that *I* had done that. At the moment that I had been watching in fascination, I was not an individual *I*, but stayed as *being.* At first, I started from the memory of *poppy flowers*, but I gradually went beyond the memory and entered their real-life magnificent, delicate beauty, finally being in Presence.

For such a person, nothing can be a *problem.* This is because this person is bigger than the problem. When you exist as an individual, you have lots of problems. However, all problems are *individual* and have nothing to do with the whole. If you could go beyond memory and reach the universe of *gamgak*, where there is no feeling of separation, you would just exist without any problems. Thus, even if you did have problems, you would still live as a person with inner peace. You know this. Although you feel afraid, lonely, upset, and frustrated, you can still live happily and pleasantly. Furthermore, you will definitely realize an obvious truth, which is that all those things are just minor, individual feelings that have no effect on the huge umbrella of *being.*

Individuality depends on *separation.* However, we usually do not feel individual and detached in our daily life. In other words, we only do so when we are fascinated with a beautiful landscape or absorbed in our work—things that don't contain a sense of *you* or *I.* Nevertheless, we *think* that *we exist.* You may think this way— maybe because you have not thoroughly looked into your state of being. You just *trust* the assumption that you exist. This is similar to a situation in which a person who has not been to Busan hears that there is a city called Busan from a lot of people, and just trusted that this was a fact. He has never been to Busan. He doesn't know what Busan is like. However, he just trusts that because almost everyone says that there is a city called Busan that Busan exists. Furthermore, he himself began to insist that Busan exists. However, does it? When he actually went to Busan, there was land, water, and mountains, not that different from other places. There were people and houses. He saw that people had drawn a line on the land and *named* the land *Busan*. At last, he realized that a specific place named Busan does not exist, but that it is just a concept on a map visualized by lines drawn for convenience.

Now, do you really trust that such a thing as *I* exists? Or did you just get to believe that *I* exist because you're called by your *name* and because you were brought up to trust that different names mean different beings? Have you ever truly explored your inner self? Have you truly discovered a separated individual there? Have you discovered an *I* possessed of unique characteristics? The reason why you regard yourself as a separated being is due to the *sense of separation*, which is just a feeling, a temporary phenomenon. It is a temporary happening of being created by our six senses, which are the five standard physical senses and the sense of our mind. Now, through the exercise on the next page, we will try to move back and forth between the state with and without a sense of separation. What you need to pay attention to is feelings. You might feel a sense of separation that you exist individually, and you might remember later on that the sense of separation disappeared momentarily and that you were immersed in the whole. Examine where your being is when you are in between.

EXERCISE 9

- Open your left hand and put it on your heart. Then, raise it so it hovers five centimeters above your chest.
- Open your right hand and hold it very close to the back of your left, not touching.
- Move your hand back to your chest, feeling the lightness that you felt in Exercise 7, The Sea of Energy.
- Amplify your inner feelings, feeling pleasant and energetic, shaking your body from side to side.
- Keep going for over 20 minutes.
- If you find that this doesn't work well, put your hands on your forehead, chest, and abdomen one by one and continue to practice on the area that gives you the strongest feeling.
- Note how the sense of being appears and disappears.

GAMGAK

Modern science and philosophy often try to persuade us—albeit confusedly—to explain the relationship between consciousness and the world. This is summed up by the following quote from Maurice Merleau–Ponty: "The world is inseparable from the subject, but from a subject which is nothing but a project of the world, and the subject is inseparable from the world, but from a world which the subject itself projects."

Philosophers use reason and scientists use experiments to explain that these two can never be separated. However, the most important thing is to ask, "Can we live peacefully and vividly through the link between the subject (self) and the world?" No matter how reasonable explanation is given, it cannot change your life.

Thus, we need insight to change the direction of our lives. We need to *deal with sensations*, which is a technique that can make progress in changing the direction, we need to recover from the traces of the past that are engraved on our body and mind and make the process slow.

The Discovery of *Gamgak*

Gamgak consists of five physical senses and the additional meta-sense that makes us experience these five senses. This meta-sense is similar to conscious awareness, but it has inner sensation. Through this inner meta-sense, the five physical senses become conscious to us as knowing. This is *gamji*.

For instance, let's say that you hear the sound of a clock. However, it is not your ears that hear the sound. Ears just interact with sound and convey its reception to the brain. At this moment, memory activates. The result is the sound being interpreted as that of a clock. This interpretation, a combination of memories, ripples towards the screen of pure consciousness, and this ripple is immediately recorded and becomes the part of the memories that you will use again later. At the same time, the label called *I* sticks to it and the thought "I know it" follows. Like this, knowing is re-experiencing. This is the process of using *gamji*. Here, memory means recalling and re-experiencing stored experiences.

If you feel a moment of discomfort or pain, take a look. Do you realize that this, too, is memory? Sensation (*gamgak*) is always different at any given moment. Using *gamgak* is like experiencing rain as individual drops of water. In contrast to this, in the case of using *gamji*, everything is stored as a whole, a collective. Therefore, while rain is really countless individual raindrops, through *gamji*, we experience it as long single rain streaks.

I is a kind of meta-*gamji*, or cognition. When *gamji* (memories), which are primarily traces of the past, form a network and shake each other, *gamgak* watch their collective movement. Every emotion is a phenomenon that comes from the relationship between *gamji*. However, the act of animals sensing and trying to protect themselves along with their internal movement is a network of *gamgak*. There is little *gamji* there, just a natural way of things. Other than pets and socialized animals, animals experience almost no distortion of reality caused by *gamji*. Through secondary sensations (*gamji*), emotions such as fear, joy, and sadness occur, and later meta-*gamji* (higher *gamji*) called *me* that integrates all of these emotions occurs. Thus, after primary sensations (*gamgak*) create a network in the field of pure consciousness, common concepts are extracted and tertiary *gamji*, the higher meta-*gamji*, are created.

After experiencing the empty universe, a black hole of no self, you are now ready to enter the universe beyond experience—you are on the last stair that you could walk up through experience. Now, you just need to leap off the last stair—you cannot go further through experience. In other words, you will enter a world where there is no longer an *I* on which to support yourself.

In the process of reaching this state, at first, you feel like you are being sucked into a black hole, but this feeling will soon pass. Eventually, all you will feel is emptiness, nothingness. This is the last experience that there is. However, we cannot remain in this state for our entire lives. We need to go beyond the experience of nothingness in order to experience daily life, always being aware that the nothingness exists. It is done at the end.

At this stage, it is important to note that you must stay in the state of *gamgak* since *gamji* cause distortions.

To find pure consciousness, you must determine whether there is a feeling of *gamji* (memory) in pure existence. However, since some subtle memories may not be detected at first, you cannot tell whether they are memories or not. Nevertheless, your consciousness becomes more fine-tuned, you will eventually sense subtle memories. For instance, right now, you cannot identify the feeling of nothingness, but later you will be able to. Then you will realize that the feeling of nothingness is also a kind of memory and stand in the way of pure consciousness.

What we call concern, worry, and anxiety are secondary feelings. At first, we just use *gamgak* to see something the way that it is. Primary *gamgak* are like the feeling of watching gentle waves shining in the sunlight, and secondary *gamji* are like the feeling of peace, comfort, and relaxation that comes shortly afterwards. In other words, peacefulness at present moment appears due to the previous contrary experience of rough waves and sly winds. Thus, *gamji* are called secondary.

Memories cannot exist by themselves. They depend on other memories. Memory X depends on memory Y and memory Y depends on memory Z and so on. In other words, your memory of a telephone depends on your memories of other things such as buttons, antennae, transmitters, and receivers. These other memories depend on other memories and the web continues to encompass more subtle memories and finer associations. The microenergy depends on more subtle energy. Finally, if you follow this web deep enough, there will be only empty space. If you look at this space, you will notice that you have been always free from memory. This is because from the beginning X and Y were unknown values, derived from emptiness. Originally, X and Y were not fundamental ideas, but temporary ones formed by pointless and short-lived changes of energy. At the root of all *knowing*, there is just *the unknown*.

Emotions are generated from specific thoughts and their associations, i.e. the relationships among secondary *gamji*. The lighter an intense emotional color is, the closer it is to being primary *gamgak*.

The feeling of *I* is also a memory. It feels like touching something with your hands, like joy and like sadness. Just as you feel things that are called physical and emotional, you feel something called *I*. All these things come and go, and don't last for ever.

First of all, in order to know the object called *you*, you must depend on the feeling of a subject called *I*. Most fundamental thing connecting a subject to an object are *gamgak—gamji* are created based on this sensory information and then causes interference. Thus, in order to deal with the many serious problems caused by *gamji*-distorted images, it is necessary to return to the intrinsic *gamgak*. Using *gamgak* means using what you feel through your sensory organs. It is feeling something as it is, not distorted by memory. However, we have lost this ability. In this book, we first practice knowing through our sense (*gamgak*), i.e. catching the pure feeling. When we can catch the pure feeling exactly, we realize that we always look at things in a twofold way. One is a sensory pure feeling and the other is *gamji*, the traces of objects that we have sensed before and the feeling of knowing that results from comparing them with each other. Therefore, we call *gamji* secondary. Every emotion occurs through *gamji*. In other words, emotion is a tertiary state caused by the relationships between secondary *gamji*. If we can feel the pure, primary feeling that is the state of *gamgak*, we can see without falling into every emotion that occurs through secondary *gamji*. This is the power of being awake.

To recap, every emotion is caused by the secondary *gamji*, the unconsciously established *criteria* from primary *gamgak*. Since being awake means you can feel the primary *gamgak*, you will come to no longer rely on the secondary *gamji* and, naturally, not be swayed by the tertiary stage called emotion.

People who are awake see objects in a twofold way: as a primary sensory object that is visible only in present moment, and as a secondary perceptional object that is the product of the past and future. However, neither sensory nor perceptional objects are real. This is because, even when seeing something through *gamgak*, there is no such thing as an individual object, and when seeing them through *gamji*, what we see are not even objects, just images inside ourselves.

Since people who are in the state of being awake see their inner mind as the state of being awake, they react purely to things through *gamgak* rather than falling into *gamji* and reacting automatically. This reaction is like seeing cosmic movements when shifting your perspective to the macroscopic universe. This is because primary senses form an organic cooperation system in which the entire universe revolves around one mechanism and everything affects each other. In this context, it can be said that there is no separate and independent existence in this universe.

Once you realize this, you will notice your waking life and dreaming life take on the same quality. You will realize that the idea of *I am* and the idea of *me* knowing something as well as the idea of *my* consciousness inevitably means that you are in a virtual world. The virtual world makes up a long continuous story. But the world of *gamgak* has no place for a story.

It becomes obvious that you are entering another dream the moment you open your eyes in the morning and notice that *you are in a bedroom*. This is because it is clearly just another plot point. Would it be possible to be in this dream, but not of this dream? This possibility begins with knowing that this world, which we believe is our waking life, is just a dream.

The moment you see *soap* in the bathroom, it becomes obvious that you are in a dream. This is because there is no soap in the universe of *gamgak*. There is just a slippery, hard, scented object. Although, of course, the concepts of slipperiness, hardness, fragrance, and objecthood itself are also just concepts.

What does it mean that thoughts are experienced? To understand this, you first must know what the nature of experience is. Let us learn about experience through touch. When putting your hands on a table, you might experience coldness. Experience, here, refers to know coldness by feeling it. Coldness is state of *gamji*, secondary. In other words, it is a concept. Concepts are memories that are refined and defined through the accumulation of many similar *gamji*. Before a concept forms, if you feel something while in the state of being awake, it will feel bare. Anyway, experience refers to know things by feeling them. In other words, it refers to inner reactions occurred when something comes into contact with our senses, namely eyes, ears, nose, tongue, skin, and mind. Therefore, it can be said that there is always a primary experience and a secondary experience. The primary experience is what feels bare through all our senses, and the secondary experience is what feels cold. Thus, prior to the secondary experience, the primary *gamgak* is the indescribable *feeling as it is*, new and different at every moment, like the touch of a newborn baby.

It can be said that thoughts can also have *primary and secondary experiences at the same time*. The primary aspect of *gamgak* is what is felt when thoughts appear and disappear on the screen of consciousness, and the secondary aspect of *gamji* is that those thoughts create a story with certain meaning and context. After all, a meaning is a secondary feeling produced by the relationship between thoughts.

Therefore, we can feel even our thoughts primarily just as we sense objects as they are. In daily life, there are times at which we feel confused when repeatedly pronouncing a certain word, even if we know it well. While repeating a word like "mother," you get the feeling, at some point, not of your mother that you've experienced or conceptually felt, but of a mere *sound* that feels unfamiliar or strange. When this happens, we witness the elimination of concept.

Concepts have inseparable and vague parts, like a continuous spectrum of colours in rainbow. However, the concept of *fire*, for example, came from many instances of actual fire. Nevertheless, the concept does not encompass every *individual real fire* there was, taking into consideration their warmth and brightness and distance. In the same way, *I* is also a concept. Just as the consciousness distinguishes this tree from that tree while extracting a common factor from both to create the concept of a tree, the concept of *I* is created when we distinguish one experience from another while finding the commonality among all our experiences.

Let me give you a simple example. *I* look at an apple that is external to me. However, am I really looking at an apple? No. In fact, there is no apple. It is just a part of the inseparable matter of the whole universe. Nevertheless, if an apple that seems to be separated from the whole is seen by *me*, it is an *apple* that is felt and experienced only in the world of *I*, which consists of *my* experiences and knowledge. Thus, the meaning and feeling of an apple differ greatly for different people. Some people, in rural areas, might grow their own apples, but others in big cities might only find apples in supermarkets or a department stores. Like this, even though the word is the same *apples* are all different, and in the strictest sense, the apple that I am looking at belongs only to me. In other words, "my apple" can be used only when combining *I* with *apple*. Thus, the feeling of "my apple" is the combination of my overall feeling of apples (the concept of an apple) that I have experienced, and my attitude, judgement, and preference about the apple (the aspect of *I*). Therefore, we have no choice but to say, "my apple."

Like this, the *reality* we experience is each of our *own* realities. Let's say that three people are standing at Seoul Station at the same time. They must feel different since A just arrived there from his small hometown, B has been on the street for 10 years, and C has returned home after a long time abroad. The *I* that A feels sees Seoul Station as busy and fast-moving compared to his slow life in the countryside. The *I* that B feels sees Seoul Station as his usual cold, stone bed, a place where it is hard to live. The *I* that C feels sees Seoul Station as shiny and gorgeous compared to 20 years ago. Each of them experiences Seoul Station differently. Therefore, every single object that one sees already consists of one's *I*. The conceptualized *I* as a whole, extracted from each *I* included in all visible objects, is the feeling of consistent *I*. The conceptualized common feelings from all the experiences in your mind and body form *I*. However, just as every concept has vague boundaries, so does the concept of *I*.

Every experience produces by-products, i.e. memories, and all memories have a small name tag that reads "I-object." These create one huge world. This is the concept of *I*.

Concepts do not really change unless real life changes. For instance, in the primitive era, fire meant bonfires, thunderstorms, or wildfires. Thus, the concept of fire included the characteristics of those things. However, life in modern society has changed a lot in terms of fire. Nuclear power is a kind of fire, and electric light is also a kind of fire. Liquids such as petroleum are also a direct source of fire. In the past, it would be unimaginable that a liquid, such as petroleum, could be like fire. As life and times have changed, so has the concept of fire.

Therefore, it can be said that concepts also live and change. The units of thought that are materials for a concept can exist only in situations where thoughts continuously flow one after another. This is because all thoughts are interconnected, like twins. They were all born in the world of non-duality. If an idea feels like fragmented and stands independently, it will soon disappear. However, since thoughts, and by extension concepts, are all connected, with this one explaining that one and that one defining this one and so on, they can exist only if constantly moving from this to that. But, if you can feel a thought by using *gamgak*, the thought as a concept will immediately stop and you will not be affected by it. This is because you will resist being captivated by the content of the thought, just noticing it as a kind of an object of experience that came into contact with your screen of consciousness.

The world of *gamgak* has no boundaries. Only when you enter the world of *gamji* do boundaries and separation and discernment occur. This is why thought loses its power and disappears when it enters the world of somatic sensory *gamgak*.

** For more on *gamgak*, please refer to Being Awake Testimonials, "The Boundary between Thought and Feeling" on page 217. This experiential story explains *gamgak* in detail and can enhance your understanding of them.

Now, let's try a comprehensive exercise. Go to the marketplace and start practicing with objects and plants, targeting their colors and scents. Firstly, feel the silence in and around the target object. See and feel the object and distinguish your memories of it from the object itself. Feel the difference between the memory and the feeling of the real object. Memory is a feeling of familiarity or of knowing. For instance, find a speaker. Look at its square shape. At this point, the feeling of *square* is just based on memory. Find out where the memory is felt in your body. Then, remove it and look at the speaker again.

If this goes well, practice on several objects with all five senses. Practice the same while watching, touching, listening to, smelling, and tasting them. If they *feel known* or familiar, practice identifying the memory behind this feeling. In other words, while looking at and feeling objects, see if you can determine what is *memory* and what is *present*, and stay *present*. Do this by looking at different things, listening to different sounds, smelling different scents, tasting different tastes, and touching different things.

Let's move on to emotions. Choose an emotion that you experience often. Recall the moment that you felt this emotion most strongly or for the first time. It is important to realize it, especially in the case of trauma, since trauma which evokes shocking emotions due to negative experiences usually belongs to the past. Go back to the moment when the emotion stuck to your body and identify it. Understand that although you feel it regularly, that is just you re-experiencing the past whenever a similar situation occurs. In other words, notice that you are feeling stored memories. This exercise covers anything related to the seven passions, namely joy, anger, sadness, fear, love, hate (disgust), and lust. However, since *anger* is a very strong emotion, it is difficult to notice that it is a re-experience. Anger tends to captivate us and hinder our perception. However, it is definitely an emotion of the past. If it is familiar and known to you, it is already stored in memory. If you feel rather dull or blank than angry, practice on feelings of dullness or indifference. These are also based in memory. Continue this exercise with all emotions, such as shame, regret, boredom, anger, pleasure, displeasure, and a sense of loss. (Feeling afraid of going through the same again after being heartbroken by losing something in life.)

Now, turn your attention around and locate silence. Focus on the fact that emotions are things remembered. While doing so, try to figure out which emotion shakes up your mind the most and isolate it. Additionally, remove things remembered as powerful feelings in your body by observing them, while noticing that subtle feelings are also memories. Observe yourself like this. At this moment, you might feel unpleasant feelings rising inside you. Feel their energy level and where they are in your body. This is the feeling of the body. Distinguish the feeling of knowing or familiarity from these feelings. Then, turn your attention to the here and now and realize that these feelings have little to do with the present moment. Note that what you are feeling is just stored memory. Just by looking at it, it will disappear and your mind will regain strength. This is because the fact that you can see them means you are becoming conscious. You are waking up. These unconscious and autonomous processes do not work in hiding. Once you can see them, you are well on your way to being awake.

** Caution: let go of your preconceived notions of the word *feeling*. Touch an object and distinguish between the feeling of knowing (*gamji*) and the pure feeling as it is (*gamgak*). To see if you can distinguish it like that, ask yourself as follows: can you tell the difference between thought, *gamji*, and *gamgak*?

Expansion

We live by limiting ourselves to our body. Because of this, we feel like we are *in* our body. But if we allow ourselves to go beyond these limits, our *I* will be able to get infinitely bigger and smaller. We can start to experience the expansion of *I* by stopping identifying ourselves with the body and starting to identify with *energy*, which is itself capable of infinite expansion. The feeling of *I* can identify with anything. For example, when you drive, you identify with your car. This is how you are able to drive without accidents. If you didn't identify yourself with your car, you wouldn't be able to feel things like your speed, the road conditions, the distance between other cars, and if you're turning safely. By identifying with your body's capability to unconsciously process and react to more than 10 million stimuli per second, you can drive a car as if it were your body. Thus, ever since you were born, you have been practicing *identifying with your body* through trial and error. We have practiced for countless hours to drive this more delicate and detailed vehicle than a car. As a result, we walk on two legs, freely use our hands, and speak with fine tongue movements. In addition, when we feel threatened, we deal with the threat by identifying with the feeling of fear and trying to remove the threat through the feeling of anger. The reason why all these things are possible is because the process of identification unconsciously happens inside of you.

By learning to identify with your thoughts and consciousness, you can use the concept of *I*. Most of the time we identify with our own bodies and minds, but when we watch a TV show or soccer match, we identify with the hero or the player kicking the ball. This causes us to deeply feel their emotions like joy, anger, sadness, and pleasure. Like this, the mind has an amazing capacity.

Yet, there is a problem: we are identified with things unconsciously, instead of identifying with things consciously and purposefully. If you were able to notice the moment you identify with something, you would be able to use it, but by not noticing it, your life force wastes a lot of energy in the process of identification.

Therefore, by practicing the exercise below, let's learn that it is not necessary to be bound to the body by taking the life force that is identified with the body and pointing it toward a greater infinite energy.

EXERCISE 11

Start with focusing on a point in front of you. Like ripples in a lake, allow the point to largen. Feel the energy grow with each ripple until it eventually wraps around you.

When you feel the energy of the wave, close your eyes, open your left hand, and bring it close to your chest. Place your right hand over the back of your left, not touching. Focus your consciousness on the center of your body and gently sway from side to side. If you feel the movement of the energy at this moment, expand it so it passes over your body, the room, and the universe. (If you feel the energy at this point, keep your hands apart at the interval at which you most strongly feel it. If you cannot feel the energy, bring your right palm closer to the back of your left hand and think of *Feeling Lightness* in Exercise 9. Take the lightness from your chest, and let it spread through your body, swaying gently as you feel the energy of lightness and joy.)

Gamgak and its Various Uses

Can you distinguish between thought, *gamji*, and *gamgak* now? Let's test it out by touching the different things below and seeing what comes to mind. If names, images, and *thoughts of knowing* these things come to mind, that is *thought*. If there is automatic *feeling of familiarity* without any thoughts, you are feeling *gamji*. If there is a pure feeling, without the thing being familiar or known, you are feeling *gamgak*. Now that you can distinguish between thought, *gamji*, and *gamgak*, now you will see everything as/with/ through them all. Let's distinguish and feel the *gamgak* and *gamji* of various objects.

> EXERCISE 12

You will need a partner for this exercise. One person should close their eyes and let themselves be led by the other.

- Lie in fresh grass or fallen leaves on the forest floor. Try to feel your surroundings without thinking or feeling that you already know it well.
- Close your eyes and let your partner guide you through a strange land. How do you feel? Do you have any sense of knowing? Do you understand now what *gamji*, the feelings of

familiarity, mean? Can you feel *gamgak* in their absence?

- Try to hold two similar but different leaves in your palm. Feel them with the back of your hand and note the differences between the two. Don't answer aloud, but can you use *gamji* to tell the difference between the feelings of the leaves? Can you use *gamgak* to find the pure feeling without *gamji*?
- Close your eyes and touch a mossy rock and a dry rock. Try to distinguish between thought, *gamji*, and *gamgak* with them.
- Look at other natural objects, both near and distant for a while and distinguish between your thoughts, *gamji*, and *gamgak*.
- Gently put your face on fallen leaves or rocks. Feel the wind and become it.
- Gently place tree branches, sand, stones, soil, grass, or spiderwebs on the inside of your wrist and feel them.
- After looking at small things, look at big things. Feel the difference between the *gamji* of the two.
- Feel the changes in your own pulse, breathing, and temperature, and try to distinguish between your thoughts, *gamji*, and *gamgak*.
- Touch and feel your hair, ears, and nose, and try to distinguish between your thoughts, *gamji*, and *gamgak*.

Seeing Unfamiliarly

Seeing unfamiliarly means seeing something as if for the first time in your life. Even when you are walking along a familiar road, there are times when you feel as if you are seeing something for the first time. And when you look closely at your face in the mirror, sometimes it starts to look strange. Even though it is the face you have always had, and the street is one you used to walk on, somehow you momentarily fail to match any information from your memory to them, so you encounter them as something new. If you can learn to escape your memory at any time and see things unfamiliarly, you will gradually find a way to go beyond *gamji* (memory) to *gamgak*.

Poets often say that *seeing unfamiliarly* is the basis of writing poems. This is because poetry is a way to the mystery beyond the universe familiar to us. It is an unknown world. In this unknown world, *gamji* stop and only *gamgak* work.

The process of seeing unfamiliarly enables us to detach the names from the things you see with your thoughts, to remove shape and quality from the things you see with *gamji*, and finally approach the world of *gamgak*. Therefore, seeing unfamiliarly takes place in the order of name removal to shape removal to quality removal.

Looking at an object, determine its name, shape, quality, and your stored knowledge of it.

- Look at an object.
- Look at it after removing its name.
- Look at it after removing its shape.
- Look at it after removing its quality.
- Look at it after removing the thought that says you are looking at it.

Meeting Objects

Have you ever been able to connect with things as they really are? For young children, it may take an hour to move just one meter on the way to the playground because they are distracted by and curious about so many different kinds of new things. This is because they focus on the so-called "here and now" and see things as they are. I remember a children's poem I heard when I was a child. In the poem, a mother sends her child to a shop on some errand, like finding out the time. The child looks around on the way, finally making it to the shop and asking for the time. The owner says, "Half past four." The child thanks him, and repeats, "Half past four, half past four" to himself all the way home so as not to forget it. However, the child sees an entire field of colorful flowers and is distracted by them for a while. After a while, his mother's errand suddenly returns to his mind, and he starts to walk again, mumbling, "Half past four, half past four" so he won't forget it. Then, he sees the vigorous leap of a fish's tail and a big splash of water. He spends some time watching fish in the river. When he starts walking again, he keeps muttering, "Half past four, half past four." This time, his eye is caught by a kite, flying around looking for prey on the ground, swooping down as if to catch something. He eventually gets home and tells his mother, "Mom, it's half past four."

Like this, almost all children live a life that is focused on the here and now, regardless of time. They are not interested in half past four. Always in the moment, they concentrate all their energy on things and become one with them easily and quickly. This is how to connect with things in a true sense. Only when we truly connect with an object can we become one with the object without being affected by our inner *gamji*.

(EXERCISE 14)

It is okay if you feel your *gamji* emerge from within during this exercise. When this happens, grasp and feel them and practice becoming one with them. The difference between the past and the present moment is that previously, you unconsciously identified yourself with *gamji*, but now, you should be able to deal with them by consciously feeling them, becoming one with them, and falling away from them, and repeating this process.

- This exercise is ideally performed outside and in nature. Go to the forest and move toward an object that attracts you. Repeat "Merge into the whole" and feel oneness with it.
- Knowing something means to be separated from it. In Exercise 13, when looking at the object after removing the thought that says you know it, there was no sense of separation. To directly enter that state, we will use the words, "Merge into the whole." The process has two steps:

1) First, approach an object or a plant, remove its name,

remove its shape, remove its quality, and finally remove the thought that says you know the object.

2) In this state, quietly speak to yourself, "Merge into the whole." Then, continuing to repeat these words, enter the state of oneness immediately.

BEING AWAKE

A relative world is a world where there are you and I, the seer and the seen, the feeler and the felt. On the other hand, an absolute world is a world that embraces and enables both subjects and objects—a world where identification with both subjects and objects is cut off.

What is Being Awake?

What does being awake mean? We can usually say we are awake at any given moment. Of course, compared to being asleep, it would make sense to say that we are awake right now. However, if you look closely at this logic, you will see that the state we believe to be waking is also a kind of sleep. In other words, just as we are unconscious and unresponsive to what happens around us when we are asleep, we are unresponsive and unconscious to the feelings of things, like a desk or a pot of flowers, when we look at them right in front of us. If this is the case, what is it that we are really seeing when looking at the flowers? We see *gamji*, traces of the *past* stored inside us. When we recognize something, we almost always fail to feel the way the object exists. Due to varied experiences, you only see the festival of images that were added to the *flowers* you sense through *gamgak*. Thus, it is more accurate to say that right now, we are not awake. We are asleep, with little thought of waking up because we are fascinated by the festival. However, the festival also causes confusion and suffering because of its constant disturbances, which leads you to set out on an epic road in hopes of escaping it. Thus, when finally, with great effort, you realize that you are, in fact, asleep, you will be able to see visible objects in two ways. One is its pure state, which is *seen* as the state of *gamgak*, and the other is what you *see* through *gamji*, which is a network of images that have piled up inside you throughout your lifetime. When you become awake, you will be able to freely see these two different sides of every object.

As we have seen so far, there are different levels and stages to the state of being awake.

First, as mentioned above, there is being awake to objects as they are through *gamgak*.

Secondly, going further, there is being awake to the fact that even a sensory feeling is just a *phenomenon* that occurs in the field of pure consciousness.

Thirdly, there is being aware that you being able to stay awake is enabled by the source of consciousness, and being one with the source.

I expect you to learn to distinguish between *gamji* and their preceding *gamgak* as well as feel the state of *being* through the being awake exercises in this book. The most important aim of this book is to recognize the difference between *gamji* and *gamgak*, to experience waking consciousness, and to be freed from identification. However, in order to switch from using *gamji*, which are a kind of image of the past, to *gamgak*, it is necessary to set aside everything you've known—not only the *names* of things but also their *shapes* and *qualities*—and taste everything as it is. So far, in order to achieve this, we have variously examined and felt attention, which is a conscious aspect of life force, and also distinguished between *gamji* and *gamgak*. Finally, let us enter the state of being awake.

When you are awake, you will experience a thought stopping by itself for the first time in your life. For the first time, you will hear *sound* instead of *speech* that is full of images and meaning. Even when you are listening to sound as is and the meaning of it is understandable, you will hear the *speech* and the *sound* of the speech at the same time. For ordinary people, experiencing these two dimensions at the same time is an impossible phenomenon— how can you be in two different dimensions at once? However, for people who are awake, it is possible. They now see *light* and *objects* at the same time. This is because it is possible for them to see these two dimensions simultaneously.

By the way, there is a subtle variation. Being awake is an empty consciousness, a state of being open to everything that can be sensed. However, if something goes wrong, you may feel an *image* of an empty consciousness that has no content. This is a kind of fixed *feeling* that is distinct from true emptiness. In other words, the state of emptiness and the *empty feeling* are totally different. Only when you can distinguish the two can you finally enter the state of emptiness, being awake.

EXERCISE 15

• A basic exercise for being awake.
- After paying attention to an object and feeling for *gamji* and removing them, enter the state of *gamgak*. Then, feel your consciousness paying attention like that.

– Distinguish between the attraction, the repulsion, and the dullness of attention and identify each manner. After that, in the state of being awake, feel for attraction and repulsion in your attention. Here, feeling means being awake in a neutral, passive state. See them *transparently*, without any *intention* to stop either.

- Look at an object in front of you by using *gamgak*.
- Gradually increase the number of objects that you are feeling. First feel one object and then the ones to the left and right of it. Then add the two things to the left and right of those.
  – Simultaneously feel two objects distant from each other. Every three minutes, practice with at least five separate objects, for a total of 15 minutes or more.
  – Simultaneously feel three objects distant from each other. Every three minutes, practice with at least five separate objects, for a total of 15 minutes or more.
  – Simultaneously feel the four objects distant from each other. Every three minutes, practice with at least five separate objects, for a total of 15 minutes or more.
- Finally, simultaneously feel every object around you for 10 minutes.

- Use *gamgak* on an object. Can you see it? Now, *feel* the waking consciousness that is sensing the object. Can you feel that? Hold it still. If you get sleepy, bored or the consciousness weakens during the practice, look at the object again. And be *conscious* of the consciousness seeing the object.

Feeling Waking Consciousness

In the state of being awake, there is no sense of balance or stability. This is because balance and stability exists only when the energy revolves under the centripetal force to a center, in which energy is concentrated. In other words, all our energy tunes toward the virtual center that is *I*, and when we ourselves tune into the center, we feel a sense of balance and stability.

However, in the state of being awake, there is no center. Rather, it is a state in which all kinds of center are gone, like a state of zero gravity. On Earth, if you work against the direction of gravity that pulls you toward the center of the Earth, you feel imbalanced and lose stability. The state of being awake is like that. There is nothing to attract or push you away from any thought or emotion that would normally snag your *I*. There is a just an open, empty, waking consciousness.

Then, how is the state of being awake different from one of *being conscious* or *knowing*?

In brief, knowing something means locating it within an entire system. For instance, when you get off the subway and try to leave the station, you often do not know which exit to choose. Even if there is a way you usually take, it often feels like you do *not know*. This is because a part of the whole composition is unknown to you. In other words we remember all exits, all buildings, and every location as one great relationship, a phenomenon in which knowing occurs when you recognize where the exit you want to go to is located within the entire scheme.

In addition, when this feeling of *knowing* lasts, it is considered proof that *consciousness exists* and being conscious means you are one part of a big story, a story that is a net of experience that links the *gamji* of this and that together. There are two kinds of stories. One is a fictional story and the other is a story created through experience. At this moment, can you escape from the fictional inner story? Is it possible to stop being in a story? The state of having all stories removed from your consciousness at a given time is being awake.

The *whole story* is the world that your *I* sees. The world we are looking at, that is to say, the *world* that we think we *know*, is actually a *story* that is embedded inside us. Thus, all the objects that you see in front of you are *gamji*, traces of the past, and the reality you are living is a dream, a huge fabrication, created by their network.

EXERCISE 16

1. Stop thinking. When you stop breathing, your thoughts stop, too, so hold your breath. Then, start breathing again and hold your thoughts still. When the thoughts rise back up, stop breathing again to stop them. At this time, pay attention to the *feeling* of being in a state where breathing and thoughts have stopped.

Even though all external sounds and changes are felt in such a state, pay attention to the *feeling* of it.

2. Move your consciousness toward inside. See different thoughts as they arise. Take a close look at the entire space within you. Now, see where the thoughts are located within that space. When you find the location, turn the eyes of your consciousness to the entire space. Be conscious of the whole space, not paying attention to any corner of it.

3. Discover consciousness regardless of thought.

   - Open your eyes and be conscious of the whole area around you.
   - This is called waking consciousness.
   - First, recognize what the thoughts that come to your mind are, and feel your waking consciousness that exists regardless of them.
   - After visualizing the boundary of your body, feel your body recognizing it for 10 minutes.
   - Feel waking consciousness for 10 minutes. This is not about awareness of your five senses, but simply feeling and being aware of consciousness. After understanding this, practice for two hours without stopping.
   - Look at the eyes of the guide and feel waking consciousness for at least 30 minutes.

When you start to be awake, you may feel more thoughts and emotions rising. This is a phenomenon that occurs when you gradually gain awareness of what is happening so far, which you weren't aware of at first. Therefore, there is no need to consider this a failure. Since it is a more subtle phenomenon, you should consider it proof that you can be aware of what you have missed so far. The important thing now is to focus on waking consciousness to more inner objects, not on more inner objects themselves. Thus, always direct your attention to *waking consciousness itself that feels objects.*

When seeing unfamiliarly, a common phenomenon in the beginning is that things appear to stick out to you, seeming to be the only things in sight.

In addition, you might become unaffected by thoughts and emotions that you normally had difficulty controlling. For example, a broad-minded student with a strong sense of justice and anger problems might become able to catch thoughts as they arise and prevent himself from being affected by them. Catching thoughts the moment they arise means that you have already emerged from the state of *being lost in thought, being one with it.* In the past, you unconsciously merged with thoughts as they arose, letting your energy flow into them, but now, you can clearly realize that you are not the same as the thoughts and identify them when they arise. Finally, you come to see them as not yourself, but as *objects.* This allows the energy channel to be cut off.

Being Awake with Objects

Now that we have learned what being awake is, let's practice being awake with things. People often think that meditation means entering an empty world of darkness where there are no objects, no thoughts, and daily life has disappeared. If this were the case, we would not be able to live in meditation. This is because if nothing were able to come to your mind in your consciousness, you would not be able to do anything, like go to and from work. That is the literal meaning of meditation in which attention flows toward an empty darkness. However, being awake means that even though you are conscious and know of all things, you realize that there is calm and great peace behind all your *knowledge* of them. It is like knowing that all sounds are *little phenomena* that happen against an infinite background called *silence*. Being awake means that you live everyday life as usual, while simultaneously living with a pure consciousness.

To achieve this, let's practice the first exercise about being awake with things.

- Feel waking consciousness while looking at an object for 10 minutes.
  - Make sure that you immediately feel waking consciousness when feeling the object.
  - See and feel an object, and then, feel waking consciousness feeling it.
  - Speed up this process: 1) Look at an object, 2) Remove its name, shape and quality, 3) Feel it using waking consciousness. 4) *Feel* your *waking consciousness that feels it* and keep speeding up the process until you can cycle through it in an instant. Practice this for 20 minutes.

- Afterwards, practice being awake while looking at things outside for 10 minutes.

Being Awake with Thought

Once you get used to being awake with things, the next step is to practice being awake with thoughts. We have already noticed that we can be aware of objects and the enormous pure consciousness simultaneously. In other words, the arrow of consciousness points not only to *external* objects but to the *inner* world as well. Since inner thought is also a kind of *phenomenon*, you are ready to realize that the pure state of being awake is always in the background of thoughts as well as things.

No matter how many thoughts you have on your mind, and no matter how intense they are, they cannot be ripped away from pure consciousness. It is like the silence of a huge forest that embraces all the birdsong, rustling of leaves, and wind.

· Note: Before proceeding with this process, feel your thoughts and make sure you understand that they are *the past*. Realizing this means that every time you feel a thought, you understand that its familiarity comes from *having known it*, not knowing it presently.

EXERCISE 18

Feel different kinds of thoughts and explore them. Start by coming with random words, then try sentences and paragraphs.

- Come up with a thought.
- Notice that the thought is *the past*.
- Put the pastness down.
- Be one with the past.

Example 1. Repeat the word "father" and remove the feeling of having *known* this word. Since its familiarity comes from having known it, it is all about the past. Put this sense of being about the past away, and see if it still remains "father."

Example 2. Think about your fears of the future and rid these thoughts of the feeling of *familiarity*. For instance, thoughts like, "I have to do this," "Someone has to do that" can cause fear or anger. While thinking these thoughts, notice that your feelings are actually *the past* and put the feelings down. Also, be aware that the past is the past and you have nothing to do with it.

Example 3. Let's say that one of the tiles on the bathroom floor has broken. While you feel comfortable with the other tiles in their place on the floor, you feel uneasy when you see the tile that has broken off. What you feel at this moment is the concern that the tile should be attached to the bathroom floor. There are various thoughts and feelings involved in this concern, such as about how someone's feet might get hurt, how you feel uncomfortable, how it is not normal that the tile has broken off, etc. These complex feelings are often familiar because you have previously felt them. So, among them, extinguish the familiar feelings. Then find the new ones and feel them only.

Example 4. After putting an object in a place that makes you feel uneasy looking at it, notice how this feels and distinguish which feelings you are used to. When you put an object in an unstable place, you might *feel* that it shouldn't be there. Try to find the specific *feelings* that give you anxiety. Finally, after extinguishing all the familiar feelings, try being awake with only the new feelings.

- If you have a thought such as, "This should be a certain way," choose the situation that causes the most anxiety and practice thinking about an opposite situation. Example: Feelings about your likes and dislikes, feelings about social causes, etc.
- Allow many different thoughts to arise. If this doesn't work, try doing it while keeping your eyes open.
- Come up with a thought, feel the sense of the past it contains, and then feel the waking consciousness that exists in spite of it for 5 minutes.
- Notice that having a thought in itself is feeling waking consciousness. Practice this for 10 minutes.
- Next, keep feeling waking consciousness. At this time, every time a thought comes to you, repeat the process above.
- Simultaneously be aware of your thoughts and feel your consciousness that is not affected by them.
  - After recalling events from the past that comfort you, simultaneously be aware of your thoughts and feel your consciousness that is not affected by them.
  - After recalling events from the past that unsettle you, simultaneously be aware of your thoughts and feel your consciousness that is not affected by them.

Being Awake with Emotions

Be Free from Emotions That Are Difficult To Escape

You are in a mood. For instance, people who practice awakenment or meditation often experience regret when they unconsciously get angry. When this happens, feel the regret as it is, and at the same time feel your *waking consciousness* that is aware of it. Now, whether you feel these two feelings at the same time or one by one (although, simultaneity is false, generally felt when two things are felt in quick succession—if you really feel two things at the same time, they are not two, but one) the fact that there are two feelings means that they can be distinguished by a spatial gap or time difference between them. Carefully feel both. The fact that the feeling of regret and of waking consciousness being conscious of it coexist means that the two are distinct from each other, and being distinct means that the two are separated. Notice what separates these two. Then, move your attention towards your waking consciousness. If that goes well, send 70 percent of your attention toward waking consciousness and 30 percent toward the background that makes it possible. That means sending the arrow of attention simultaneously to the object called *waking consciousness* and the *unknown* background that makes it possible. This is, essentially, an arrow that is fired externally and internally at the same time. When we do this, our thoughts stop, and we gradually move toward the source. This is because the mind actually cannot do two different things at the same time. In addition, in this process, we naturally move away from emotions and move to the source of consciousness, which is the background of emotions. The important thing here is not to see or feel the source, but to recognize that you are it. All you can do is just experience emotions from the point of view of the source, not see or *know* the source.

Being the source of consciousness is the foundation of waking consciousness without conscious contents, and it is also the state from which we can gain awakenment. Actually, the word "gain" is not totally correct. We do not gain waking consciousness. Rather, we realize that through the source, through waking consciousness, all emotions and thoughts are possible.

It is as if we feel our attention moving from the big waves (emotions and thoughts) to deep, calm currents (consciousness), and gradually sinking even deeper. At some point, we submerge ourselves into the source itself, which feels like the entire entity of the water. In the water, we always realize that even thoughts, like rough waves, are felt in the expansive silence of the water. Therefore, in the state of being awake, there is no need to avoid such thoughts and feelings. Realize that they are just rough waves made of water and no matter how rough they are, they cannot escape from the *water*.

So now, let us feel the traces of those feelings while existing as the vast awakeness that embraces all feelings.

Being awake with emotions

- Think about a negative experience that made you angry. Feel the anger and at the same time, feel your waking consciousness that is not affected, only *knowing* the anger.
  - Start with a minor incident.
  - Then, practice with an experience that caused a great and deep anger.

  ※ If you fall into the anger and cannot control yourself, go back to feeling things, and follow the steps such as being awake with things, being awake while being conscious of your body, being awake while being conscious of everything around you, and feeling waking consciousness in turn.

- Next, think about an experience that gave you joy, and feel joy and happiness. At the same time, feel your waking consciousness that is not affected by it.
  - Start with a small or simple moment of joy or happiness.
  - Then, practice with an experience that gave you great and overwhelming joy.

  ※ If you find that you want to indulge in pleasure, go back to feeling things, and follow the steps such as being awake with things, being awake while being conscious of your body, being awake while being conscious of everything around you, and feeling waking consciousness in turn.

※ If you feel anxiety, feel that waking consciousness exists with it at the same time.

** Here's a simple way to free yourself from internal conflicts. Earnestly repeat the words below to the source of universe and the source of yourself.

· I will follow truth.
· I will do good.
· I will see beauty.

Truth gives us a thrill. The universe follows the law of truth, which works for everything without exception regardless of time and space, and it applies to not only all things but also our inner world. When following the law of truth, our minds can breathe and find deep peace. Recall a moment when you think you took a glimpse of the truth, and fill your mind with the *feeling* of the truth.

Goodness warms and moves the heart. When we feel fear, we become violent and destructive. On the other hand, when we feel safe, we become relaxed, comfortable and easy-going. Therefore, let go of fear, embrace everyone, and quietly and firmly tell yourself and your neighbors that you will do your best to do all good you can. Think of the goodness that you have experienced, fill your mind and body with the feeling of it, and then say the words.

Beauty excites us. Summon the *feeling* of magnificent beauty of this universe, the subtle beauty of nature, and the enchanting beauty of humankind. Fill your whole being with beauty. Look for beauty in everything you see.

Being Awake with the Five Senses

A person who has overcome difficulty is someone who has overcome their own *self*. This means overcoming *identifying with the I* who they believed themselves to be. This also means that they have overcome *self-memory*, and therefore, unconsciously reached enlightenment. Therefore, it can be said that people who manage to do *whatever* they once felt they *could not do* are the ones who are capable of facing their memories. However, since facing your memories is mostly done unconsciously, this rule cannot be applied to everything.

The difference between a person who has overcome difficulties this way and a spiritual seeker is whether they did so in the state of being awake or not. An awakened person knows that self-memory is a kind of limit that can be overcome at any time. All memories can be useful. Memory matters only when you are bound by it. All problems occur when you identify yourself with your memories.

Take a look at some leaves outside. There are, of course, no actual leaves there. When you see a leaf, you are actually seeing the *semantic memory* of trees, color of green, growth, sunlight, and photosynthesis. When you look at leaves, you can actually sense only its color and texture as primary (physical) sensation. Everything else is memory. Of course, even primary sensations are not free of memory, as they include genetic memory.

Now, let's practice with pain. Think of a pain that comes and goes but is often felt in your body. Get rid of the feeling of familiarity and feel it again. Since your memories do not exist at this moment, you can make the pain disappear. If you do not succeed, identify the familiar feeling from the past and enter the core of it. The deeper into the feeling you go, the more you will feel that it is empty and insubstantial.

- Let's go back to pain. This time, you need to feel actual pain, not just a memory. Lift some weights or do push-ups as much as you can typically endure, keeping track of how many you do. After a short break, try to do the same exercise in the state of being awake. If pain occurs, immediately recognize the *gamji*, throw away the memory of pain, and try to stay awake only to the part that is actually felt at the moment. Count how many times you succeed at this and compare it to the first step of this exercise.

- Assume a strict posture, one that is uncomfortable yet correct, such as sitting up straight or the squat hold. Feel your waking consciousness that is not affected by the discomfort you feel.
- Practice with scent.
  - While smelling a soft and subtle scent, without falling into it, and feel your consciousness that is not affected by it.
  - While smelling a strong and irritating scent, at the same time,

feel your waking consciousness that is not affected by it.

- Practice with sound.
  - While listening to soft music that you like, feel the sound and feel your consciousness that is not affected by it.
  - While playing a strong and stimulating sound, feel it and feel your consciousness that is not affected by it.
- Practice with taste, and at the same time feel consciousness.
  - Try a bland food you like, and feel your consciousness that is not affected by it.
  - Try a strong and stimulating flavor and feel your consciousness that is not affected by it.
- Look at something new and feel your consciousness that is not affected by it.
  - While regarding beautiful scenery or a picture that gives you comfort, feel your consciousness that is not affected by it.

Feeling that *I Am*

The fact that as consciousness gets clearer, objects seem to fade away, or that the more you remain awake the less you are aware of anything else is evidence that you are getting closer to the source. For instance, if physical objects and emerging thoughts are clearly visible to us, we are not only obsessed with them but also far from the source. This is because we are looking at our own projections of a virtual *world* in which things are distinguished and separated. We project, pouring our life force into that virtual world.

Next, if the feeling of *I* is weaker than the feelings from objects and thoughts, but is still clearly felt as an object, you are still obsessed with objects. This is another way of telling that you are far from the source. Next, the feeling of *I am* is even weaker than the feeling of *I*, or difficult to sense. When compared with physical objects, it's close to rather transparent objects than opaque and colored ones. Now, going one step further, the feeling of *being* is even more transparent and hardly sensed. The feeling of *being* is the object that is closest to the source, so if you keep feeling it, you are finally in a state in which you cannot tell if you are feeling *being* or you are *being*. There is only clear waking consciousness. We call this moment *Hoegwang banjo* (回光返照).[2]

---

2) Its literal meaning is to turn the light to reflect upon the thing it originally came from.—Trans.

In other words, it means to see the *being* of consciousness with the light of *consciousness* itself. It means that the light that illuminates everything external to you comes back and illuminates the source inside you.

EXERCISE 21

1) Direct your attention to the thoughts occurring right now. Pay attention to your thoughts and feelings.

2) Try to find the feeling of *I am*, and send attention to it.

3) Pay attention to the feeling of *being*. As the feeling of *I am* was found and being felt, it will gradually move to the feeling of *being* that is more substantial.

4) When *being* is felt, move your focus to the source that enables the feeling of *being*. Notice that *being* is being felt on the basis of *it* (impersonal subject).

5) When you understand this, now try to understand that your thoughts are also felt by *it* (impersonal subject). This includes the feelings of *I am* and *I*.

Before you can do this exercise 21, you need to identify the feeling of *I am* to begin with.

Feeling *I am*

• Goal: feeling *I am* without speaking or visualizing the words.

- Walk through a forest or wooded area
- While walking, feel that there is *I* who is walking.
- Feel your existence.
- Feel the trees.
- Feel the breeze rustling the leaves.
- Feel the sun shining down on everything.
- At this moment, feel *I am* without expressing it in words.
  - ∴ Try to find the feeling of existence, not your name or label.
  - ∴ *Being* is just *being*. It is not a father, a man, a woman, a mother, a wife, a husband, or a child.
- Awaken the *being* of yourself.

- Error correction: (The guide touches the participant's hand.) Make sure that you feel the feeling. Do not express it in words. Just feel the touch.

  ∴ Gurdjieff and Ouspenky's self-remembering experiment started out with 30 people. By the end of the first week, twenty-seven had fled. Only three remained, one of whom was Ouspenky himself. One month later, he had glimpses of *I am*. After that, he experienced *being*. By the second month, even the feeling of *being* had dissolved.

** Caution: The conviction that *I know* means you are lost in thought again. Any faith, conviction, or knowing means you are lost.

- Do you have any feelings or thoughts that say, "this is me"?

- Can you leave them behind?
- If you cannot leave them behind, ask yourself why that is. What attachment prevents you from abandoning these feelings?

Attachment, or attraction, is a human characteristic. Anything that you see often or for a long time can start to attract you. Human consciousness has a tendency to settle into things, like your child, your clothes, your house, the things you care about, and so on. However, these things are not at fault. We just need to free our mind from attachment, and use the attachment at our will. If you knew that the function of consciousness is to work through attraction, would you feel more comfortable with this fact? We gain interest over time and repeated exposure to things. This sense of interest keeps our consciousness attached. It can be said that you know something only when you have looked deeply into it, grasped the network of its relationships with other things, and understood that even its small details and invisible parts are connected to each other as a whole. How can this be possible if you are not interested in it? All great figures in history, those who have accomplished outstanding achievements, were people who developed a deep, nuanced interest in certain fields. At first, they were attracted to a certain subject, and the more they gained interest in it, the more they became attracted to it. As a result, they became great experts in their chosen subjects. Great experts are people who reached profound heights in their specialty, and furthermore, often discovered links that connected it to other fields. It is not that Leonardo da Vinci started painting and then *directed* interest in science, but that his interests *drew* him to broader realms. It was through interest and attachment. In this way, the conscious activity called knowing happens through attachment.

Again, what matters is that when you are bound by attachment, it becomes a constraint, a burden, and something that makes our life more difficult. *Interest* and *attachment* act as a double-edged sword in that the deep interest can lead to attachment and obsession, but that indifference, on the other side, is also a poison that causes ignorance. Therefore, the important thing is to let the transparent interest that does not attach to anything lead you to profound realms. By doing so, we can feel the pleasure of being unburdened, the happiness of a light heart, and the great joy that comes from the combination of the two. Joy is the feeling that occurs when the pleasure of the body and the happiness of the mind are both in full effect. When you remove *I* from this, so only joy and happiness remain, you finally can reach a state of ecstasy.

Thus, do not get used to attachment, but *use* it. Using something means you can put it down at any time. Do not avoid, do not blame, and do not be afraid.

The human consciousness can use anything. Humans can fly and be free at any time.

IDENTIFICATION

Without *intention* to know, you *could never know* anything. Once you have an intention, you send *attention* in its direction, and its position in the whole network of existence is revealed. The sense of position within the whole creates a sense of *knowing*. By then, identification has already occurred.

Going Beyond the Self as a Sum of Past Experiences

The biggest burden in life would be the sense of *I*. But it is easy to leave behind. You just have to notice that it is a feeling, a kind of memory, that appears depending on different situations. Through the exercises we have done so far, we have learned that *gamji* are traces of past experiences. Everything that feels known or familiar is *gamji*. Therefore, the most familiar feeling, *I*, is also a kind of *gamji*.

We can easily leave behind memories, though. *Gamgak* naturally occur at every moment. It involves only genetic and biological memories. It is good. Use it. However, all other memories are secondary—*gamji*—and you must be able to abandon them any time. In the end, this will include *I*, too.

George Gurdjieff spoke about being aware of oneself at all times. He called it self-remembering. He demonstrated that we always react to things in similar ways, repetitive like machines, and suggested not to forget the feeling of *I am* so that we don't react automatically. But this is not easy. We are like light switches, turning on at the simplest of motions, reacting automatically as if we ourselves had built-in switches of anger, joy, and sadness. Gurdjieff tried to break the chain of automatic reactions through practicing being aware of the feeling of *I am*. But this method proves inefficient because it is difficult to concentrate on other things in daily life when so much effort is directed towards this deliberate awareness. It works only when you put time aside to practice it.

A method that you can do every day is the practice of being aware that *everything you see is gamji, the past.* We can easily leave behind past memories. Of course, certain traumatic experiences can leave deep wounds on the body and mind and affect someone for their entire life, but most can be easily abandoned.

However, some memories are a little more difficult. If we were to rank them by difficulty, the easiest memory to forget would be one of a random person who once briefly passed you by. And the most difficult memory to lose would be the memory of *I.* However, they all can be forgotten because they are something that has been added to you. You can forget anything as long as you first identify it as a memory.

The process for every memory, whether it is easy or difficult, is the same, so if you start with an easy one and see consciously how to let go of it, you will eventually be able to move on to the concept of *I,* too.

For example, let's say you've gone bankrupt. To abandon memory here is not to forget the situation. Your *I* at the moment identifies with your *fear* of the *misfortune that will come* from the bankruptcy, which is your own *interpretation.* You just need to realize that this is mere memories. If you do so, the energy that you were wasting on the fear disappears naturally. How is fear memory? If it were not memory, you wouldn't call it fear. The fact that *you know what fear is* proves that it is a *memory created from past experiences.*

- Feel the feeling of *I* and be aware of its familiarity
  - Since all *gamji* (to know by feeling) are memories, *I* is also a kind of memory. A memory is characterized by the unchangeability. In fact, your feeling of *I* changes slightly every day. However, because the change is so fine and small to be noticed, we assume that *I* is fixed and sense (use *gamji*) our memory of it. It's like how everyday a few of the 60 trillion cells in our body die and are reborn without us being aware of it, and so we think our body is unchanging.
- Note: If you feel sleepy when you go to being awake mode, it can be that you are still immersed in memories, i.e. something you've known. Being sleepy when your body is not tired is a phenomenon that occurs when you experience no change. You don't feel sleepy when you have to think fast, but you do if you think slow or stay in one thought. Likewise, even though you think you are awake, you might have created a *memory*, a *fixed* feeling of being awake, which will cause you to be sleepy because the fixed image has no change. In other words, if you're in the *image of being awake*, you would feel sleepy, although you think you're awake. In this case, the sleepiness will disappear when you become *aware* of the fact that *something* feels same and unchanged.

⟨Procedure 1⟩

- Feel the feeling of *I* and realize that it is a kind of memory.
- Find out in which part of your body the feeling of *I* most strongly resonates. If you feel *I* in your body, you're looking at your body in your inner world.
- It is very important to be able to identify the feeling of *I*. If you find the feeling, be aware that it is also a memory, which you recollect and re-experience. Let's **distinguish** *I* **(gamji) from the pure sense of** *being (gamgak)*.

  ① Where do you feel *I* when you see something through *gamji*?

  ② Close your eyes and use *gamji* to feel where *I* is in your body.

  ③ Close your eyes and use *gamji* to feel where *I* is in your head.

  ④ The *I* is more easily felt when someone's attention is directed toward it.

⟨Procedure 2⟩

- Let go of the *I* that exists through *gamji*.
- There is no need to hold onto memory in this silent moment.
- State of *gamgak*: Perceivable but indistinguishable. Things are present as sensory stimuli, but are indistinguishable from one another.
- State of *gamji*: Everything is separate and distinct from one another. The boundary between *gamgak* and *gamji* can be ambiguous, because they are always mixed together. However,

if you pay attention to *gamji*, they remains distinct and you can stay in that state.

- Emotional state: Referring to third feelings that occur in due to *gamji* interacting with one another.

** If you can't recognize *gamji*:

- Look at an object through *gamgak* and then associate an emotion with it, such as likes or dislikes. Do this repeatedly.
- Notice when familiarity occurs.
- To move from *gamgak* to thought, you must use *gamji*. If the existence of *gamji* is accepted, it can be sought and found.

Letting go of all memories—that is what we are going to do. But leaving them behind doesn't mean returning to a blank state with no memories. It means that we start to use the memories instead of letting them use us. When we live in memory without being aware of it, we are basically being held hostage by the memory. But once you can leave it behind, you can use it freely.

It's not as hard as you might think to find out what you identify with. Basically, if you feel a certain emotion, that means you are identifying with a thought that causes that emotion. Let's take a depressed person who feels that nothing goes the way he plans for example. Modern-day depression is very serious. According to one statistic, about 300 million people in the world—five percent of the world's population—suffer from depression. It's ironic that it is especially prevalent in developed and rich countries. Where does this depression come from? Most of the time, it comes from the unconscious identification with the thought of a life without fun, a life in which strong stimulation does not occur. The human mind constantly pursues fun. Most humans are attached to the pursuit of stimuli. It's like how we pursue stronger tastes in food and drink as we get older. The nature of the human experience is that stimuli can be *felt* only when they get stronger than before. When the person in our example fails to get the stronger stimulation he craves, he creates a feeling of falling endlessly, and falls into the feeling itself.

So where does depression come from? What causes a life without fun will vary from person to person. A person who seeks wealth will be depressed by the *thought* that wealth will not come to him and that he must live on being poor. Or, on the contrary, a person who has achieved the wealth that he pursued may become depressed by identifying with the futility in the thought that there is nothing more to gain. A person who seeks wisdom and enlightenment quickly falls into melancholy due to the *thought* that his goal is yet to be achieved and he must continue to live his boring and unchanging life, day after day without hope. They all identify with their thoughts.

Ask yourself at this point, "Do I want to get out of this depression?" If you do, ask yourself, "Can I *leave behind my pursuit of wealth or enlightenment* to get out of this depression?" If you ask yourself this question, appreciating it deep in your heart, you will find yourself be freed by your question. Ask truthfully.

The *act of pursuing* wealth or enlightenment is different from the *thought of pursuing* them. If your desire is earnest, you will not be stuck in the *thought* of wanting them, but be able to start the *action* needed to achieve them. Of course, *action* here includes both external and internal action. In other words, you wouldn't just sit and be passively dissatisfied, thinking, "How can I go to Busan? Why can't I go to Busan? Why is it so difficult to go to Busan?" Rather, you could begin to take direct action toward actually going to Busan.

Earlier, we looked at the basic formula of human consciousness, the "I-you" relationship and the "I-object" relationship. Again, everything we feel that we know is a phenomenon that occurs when a "subject-object" relationship is formed in the consciousness. What does it mean to look at a refrigerator and know that it is a refrigerator? You identify with the *gamji* of a refrigerator inside of yourself, and it takes on the role of *I*. Then, the refrigerator in front of you becomes an object, and information from the object is compared to your internal *gamji* of a refrigerator, triggering the feeling of *knowing* or *not knowing*.

So, if you feel depressed, it's the *past* because you *know* it as *depression*. Everything that you feel that you know (*gamji*) are memories. Therefore, once you notice that depression is understood through memory, it's easy to get out of it. This is because it isn't something that is happening to you now, but a feeling that had been made inside of yourself. You might get scared while watching a horror movie. But as soon as you know that this fear is a memory created by a series of past images, you can get out of it at any time. Remove the familiar feelings of the past from your present depression. What remains when you let go of all the feelings of depression that you *know* is what is actually happening now. Walk confidently out of the past. The beautiful present is welcoming you with open arms and a smile. You don't have to be obsessed with the feelings of the past, don't you think?

Disconnecting the Chain of Identification (1)

So why did we start to identify? Why did nature burden us with identification? Actually, identification can be considered a great blessing given to humans by nature.

If we didn't possess the ability to identify, it would be impossible to know or separate anything. Take, for example, the cars driving along the road. When you unconsciously look at the cars, there is no distinct feeling, tension, or *knowledge* that indicates the distance between the cars. But think of one of them as your own and look again. The stronger the identification, as if you were actually driving one of the cars, the more you will begin to *feel* and *know* the sense of distance between your car and the others. You will even be able to feel the other cars' order and speed and how they interact with one another. In this way, identification is essential for our consciousness to *know* and *feel* things. In other words, *I* is a kind of *temporary energy center* that is felt by identifying with the feelings on the inside and outside of us, so that life energy grasps the whole structure. However, this center is also the main cause of obsession, attachment, and suffering. Knowing this, it is now possible to deviate from identification as needed. But the problem is that it is not easy to free ourselves from identification. In fact, this is what lies at the root of all our problems. The ability to freely use identification is a valuable tool for us to experience life as well as major necessity for the future of our humanity. The *self* is a virtual form that is essential for identification and the process of *knowing*. But now you should be able to leave it behind at any time.

For example, think about when you first learn to drive. Unlike when you sit in the passenger seat, you now feel frightened and threatened when another car comes too close to *you (your car)* because you start to identify yourself with the car. When you are driving like this, you have to know the distance between your car and others, and you experience fear and anxiety about being too close to other cars. However, this kind of identification guarantees safe driving, and without it, car accidents would happen and the roads would be overtaken by chaos. Thus, when you identify with something, you get to *know* and *feel* what you would otherwise never do.

By the way, when identifying, does it come down to just one degree of identification when we feel an object as *I*? I don't think so. This is because the range of what is believed to be me varies enormously. We can measure the identification index of our thoughts, concepts, emotions, problems, social status, etc., that we believe to contribute to *I*. For example, how much someone identifies with a company can demonstrate whether they are the president or an employee. When comparing an employee to the president of a company, their levels of identification would be very different. The identification index used here can be divided into an emotional identification index and a mental identification index for convenience.

The emotional identification index can be measured by how

emotional you feel when the company is in trouble. The president's emotional identification would be the highest, level 10, so if the company were to go bankrupt, the president would feel like he is dying, thinking about suicide, and suffering more than anyone. But employees would not; their identification level would range from one to nine, but probably not all the way to 10, the complete identification.

The mental identification index can be measured by how much one expends their daily life energy. The president uses most of his mental energy on his company. Therefore, his mental identification level can be regarded as level 10, again. All of his energy is focused on making his company great. Meanwhile, a manager might identify with a department, so if there were 10 departments, they would identify as a level of one tenth of the president's identification, and if there were 100 lower-level employees, it can be assumed for convenience that each employee would have an identification index of one percent. Of course, for a particularly ambitious employee who thinks and works like he is the president himself, his identification level with the company may be around nine. Anyway, a higher level of identification makes a worker *feel* better and *know* more about his company, and vice versa. Without identification, even if he worked hard, he would not be able to clearly make the best decisions for the company.

This is also evident when watching a TV show or a movie. When watching a TV show, if you do not identify with the main character, you aren't interested. This is because you can't *know* or *feel* the subtle relationships between the characters and how energy flows through their interactions. It is said that men find it difficult to be interested in or understand emotional TV shows as their level emotional identification is generally weak. Men or those who are not good at emotional identification cannot know the fun of TV shows. On the other hand, women who don't identify with intellectual or logical competitions are not interested in games or sports. Like this, in order to *know* or *feel* anything, identification is essential.

The most basic identification that occurs to all humans beings is the concept of *I*. The *I* has both emotional and mental aspects. It is the identification game of *you* and *I* that makes our lives interesting and dynamic. It also brings us a very desperate feeling.

The problem is that emotional and mental identification can make you feel not only interested but also in pain. You can see this reflected in times that you have been sad or distressed when the main character of a TV show is sad or faces difficulties. All this suffering comes from *identification*. So identification is the last barrier we must overcome. Only then can we use *identification* freely. In other words, through identification we *know* and *feel* the world, but at the same time, we are *restrained* in its knowing and feeling. Identification is like a double-edged sword. If you can use it for the world, you will get detailed *knowledge* and dynamic *mental feelings*, but if you are tied up in it, you will fall into suffering and agony.

So the purpose of *being awake* is to *use identification* without these side effects. In using identification freely as needed—not in escaping it unconditionally—lies the excellence of creative beings. You can used it to know and feel the world and its people, and when you don't need it, you can leave it behind. This is the ultimate goal of *being awake.*

Let's look at the process by which identification happens.

First, in order for identification to occur, it is necessary to divide ourselves into *me* and *thing that is not me*; this is *separation.* Identification cannot happen when everything is one. This is why the concept of *I* is not established in *babies* who cannot distinguish themselves from other things in the world. There can be no identification where there is no separation. That is why there is the saying that we need discrimination, but we must be able to leave it behind at any time to be free. In other words, discrimination is necessary before identification can take place. So, how does discrimination happen? When we are born for the first time and start to sense external stimuli, sensory distinction naturally occurs. In our eyes, there are cones and rods that discern the difference between colors and light, and this is recorded on the screen of our inner consciousness. Everything is not clearly documented from the beginning, but the repeated experiences, the ones necessary for survival, leave deep traces as they are considered important. These traces are called *gamji* in this book. It means to know by feeling. In Buddhism, *gamji*, images with names, and thoughts are called *samjñā* (相). They can also be called mental feelings or images. The important point is that *samjñā* (相) is a fixed and unchanging past. If *samjñā* was always changing and not constant, we would not be able to recall it. It can be used as a tool or material for thought because it is a set of fixed feelings and impressions. In this book, *samjñā* (相) is classified into first *gamji* and second *gamji* for more subtle distinction possibilities. First *gamji* are faint traces that the sensory organs leave when they sense a thing. When the sensory organs encounters the same stimulus again, these traces result in the feeling of *familiarity*. If this sensation is felt repeatedly for a long time, the clear feeling of *knowing* is created. This is the state of second *gamji*, traces that remain solid after the first *gamji* die down. When the second *gamji* pile up inside, identification with those unchanging *things* happens ceaselessly, and the feeling of *I* starts to attach itself to them, compared to other things that are changing.

The fact that humans live now means that they live by identifying themselves with a part of their *inner world*, which is made like this. This book aims to prove that the *inner world* or the *world seen by me* now is made of traces of the past that have arisen above the source consciousness, and declare that we should live by identifying with one of them as needed and then letting go of it freely.

EXERCISE 23.1

- The fact that we react means that subtle identification has already occurred.
- First, find out what thought you are identifying with.
- See what other thoughts create the reaction with the identified thought.
- The fact that you see the world now indicates that you are

identified with something. Otherwise, you wouldn't see any *world*. If there's any, it is just the undivided whole that is perceived by the senses.

When you have the intention to see something, a subject and an object arise. For example, when you open your eyes but register nothing, that means you are consciously looking at nothing even though your eyes are open. When you have the intention to see, such as curiosity or concern, you see whatever it is in front of your eyes. Similarly, when you ask yourself, "Who sees this thought?" the feeling of *I* who see the thought arises. In other words, the intention to see creates *the seer* and *the seen*.

The Power of Attention

British biologist Rupert Sheldrake claims that when we stare at something, the power of that staring can cause the thing to react. To prove it, he conducted an experiment in which staring at a human subject caused them to turn around and look back.

This may sound absurd, but he was able to prove statistical significance through this experiment. When the experimenter looked at the test subject, he asked whether the test subject had experienced a feeling of being watched. The results of the compiled experiments were not only correlation—they proved causation as well.

This is actually something we can easily test ourselves. A single mirror is enough to experience the power of attention.

EXERCISE 24.1

Needed: a small mirror or a full-body mirror with which you can see your face.

Directions: Look at your face in the mirror. In this case, the face in the mirror is the object. Now, imagine that you are looking out at yourself from inside of the mirror and turn your attention from the mirror to yourself. What do you experience?

Let's do another exercise. Before that, I would like to mention an experiment that took place in Japan in 2000. Japanese scientist Dr. Mikio Yamamoto was conducting experiments on outer qigong. He wanted to know if the radiation of qi, which we often call jangpung in Korean, was a real phenomenon. We use the term "outer qigong" here because the focus is on the aerodynamic force of qi that is expelled outwardly. In the experiment, a person who radiated qi was on the second floor of a building, and a person who receives the qi was on the first floor. When the qigongsa, the person who radiated the qi, sent it to the person on the first floor, the receiver fell down, sometimes successfully receiving the qi and sometimes not. Interestingly, when such an energy exchange occurred, the brain waves and electrocardiographic reports of the two people were in sync. This experiment showed that we always exchange cosmic energy in the form of qi and consciousness, and that this energy exchange can be very strong when two beings are in tune or resonate with each other.

Now, let's go outside and try to practice exchanging energy or microconsciousness with plants. Make sure to create an environment in which you and your plants will be in sync. To do so, use the following *consent procedure.*

EXERCISE 24.2

Go outside and approach a plant to which you feel attracted. First, look at the part of the plant that attracts you. Look at its fresh energy. Now, try to assume the perspective of the plant and look at yourself. Here are two ways of resonating with each other. The first is to *ask the plant for consent,* and the second is to *become your counterpart and look at yourself.* What experience results from this?

Disconnecting the Chain of Identification (2)

Through being awake or exercises like the mirror activity, you can experience nothingness or the infinite expansion of consciousness. However, even if you have experienced deep nothingness, identification still remains because *you identify with having such an experience.* You must escape that identification. You may have experienced nothingness, but all experiences are still centered on external *objects*, not the subject that does the experiencing. You have not yet gained insight into the *source.* So again, you fall into identification with the thought "I have experienced nothingness." No matter how deep your experience of nothingness was, *identification with an experience* is still identification with an object. You consider yourself one with the experience as you do with objects, and this soon leads to more identification. Because you don't know that you are in the state of identification, the pattern recurs. Therefore, you must see through identification itself. No experience lasts forever. All experiences are just paying attention to an *object.* All experiences, from amazing and ecstatic ones to one's nothingness are in the end just that—*experiences.* They all inevitably pass, just as all objects constantly come and go. What makes objects visible; how do you catch them? You have to focus on them.

Then how does identification happen? When you are trapped in, for example, intense anger, there is no *I* present. You don't *know* that you are angry because there is only anger. This is a unitary state. This anger is animalistic and of a child whose selfhood is yet to form. But when you start to feel and know the anger, you are divided into the *feeling of anger* and *feeling of I* who recognizes anger. From this point on, separation of self occurs, and one enters a dualistic state. To *know* that anger is not one's source, this separation is necessary. We need to endure the process of dividing our inner world in two. Only then can we truly train to be awake. So, how can we be alive to anger?

First, when you are full of anger, in order to feel it internally, you need to separate *I* from the anger so that *I* can feel the anger. This separation needs to happen temporally or spatially. In other words, after the anger passes, you need a temporal gap in order to form the *I* that can feel and know the trace left by the anger. Second, when the inner world is divided into the feeling of *I* and the *anger* itself, the anger can be noticed immediately. In this case, *I* is a feeling that suppresses or analyzes the anger. After all, feeling something only happens when the inner world is divided into various feelings. To feel means for the inner world to be divided.

Sleep is similar to anger, in a way. While sleeping, there is only subtle state of sleep, so you cannot be alive to, therefore *know*, the sleep. You are immersed in the state of *sleeping*. Only when you emerge from the sleep and the feeling of *I* begins to appear do you *remember* or *know* that you had been asleep. Therefore, when you are full of sleep or full of anger, there is no *I* to know what is happening at that moment.

If there is *I* to know that you are angry or sleeping, this is because you are divided into anger and *I*, or sleep and *I*. So, knowing that you are sleeping in your sleep or knowing that you are dreaming while dreaming means that you are already divided. In these processes, you identify with something divided.

Above all, what is important is to escape identification.

EXERCISE 25.1

- Notice a feeling that you have. Be aware that the process of you feeling it is a process toward division.
- When you are full of something like anger or sleep, which we will call A, you don't feel anything. When anything secondary, B, is created, *feeling* results. In other words, only when you are divided can you *know* or *feel*.
- Focus on finding the feeling that arises when you say "father" or "mother." If you feel attracted to or repulsed by it, that means there is an *I* present to react to it. How do you know that you feel it? You should know that knowing is also a kind of sensation, like something you can taste or smell. It can be said that reason is a sensation, too. It is the same as in Buddhism that when the sensory organs (the eyes, ears, nose, tongue, body, and mind, 眼耳鼻舌身意) sense things such as color, sound, smell, taste, touch and dharma, which includes thoughts (色聲香味觸法).

Practice feeling *I* and putting it down. Only when you feel *I* can you put it down.

- Having or being conscious of a feeling means that you are already identified with something. So, a thought that is between the separate two, whether it is one of repulsion or attachment, comes, and a feeling appears as the reaction to it.

- The "middle way" means not to stand on either side by identifying. In other words, it means to be neutral.

- This constant need for your *I* to be present, a certain tendency that forms your *I*, is also a phenomenon of existence. It has a cosmic force to maintain itself. If you can see identification happening, you can escape it.

Waves move constantly, but the nature of water doesn't change. Move your attention to this unchanging characteristic. Consciousness moves constantly and can be quite dramatic. However, be aware that its innate properties remain unchanged.

What does it mean when we say that *kleśa* are *bodhi*, perfect enlightenment? It means that we should focus on the quality of consciousness, not the shape of it. All the contents of consciousness derive from the shape of consciousness. Forget the shape that your consciousness is taking at the moment and pay attention to its quality. Consider its contents as waves and its quality as water and pay attention to the water.

Every instance of identification is energy attaching itself to the shape of consciousness. Since shapes are different, they cause the separation of *you* and *I*, which naturally results in various emotions. When you disregard the shape of consciousness and focus on its quality, you will notice what in consciousness is unchanging.

However, we must not forget that separation and discrimination is not in the nature of objects, only occurring through the function of consciousness. Things are not separated originally. *Separation* is merely an addition, something that we project onto objects in order for our human consciousness to have the experience of knowing. If things were separated fundamentally, all of nature and the universe wouldn't show signs of connection between them. Everything would exist on their own, and the law of causality, "Because there is this, there is that," would never have existed. The universe has never been divided in the first place, but human consciousness has divided and named things, just to say that there are connections between the divided things.

It's like cutting a piece of watermelon into rind, flesh, and seed, and saying that there is an inevitable relationship between the three components. Watermelons have never been divided in the first place, and therefore there is no inseparable relationship between their components—they were all one thing to begin with.

The process of identification is a ridiculous process. It's a virtual device created purely by our consciousness in order for it to make sense of the world.

If you see and listen to an object without the feeling of *I*, the object will disappear, which is using *gamgak*—that is, to see things as they are without attraction or repulsion.

In religion, vertical and horizontal relationships coexist. A vertical relationship is when you use other people for your own benefit, and a horizontal relationship to understand how both you and others move. Religion, in the future, should follow a horizontal path that seeks to understand even the most subtle of movements between the two parties.

Abandoning the Sense of Emptiness

When you learn to use *gamji*, you realize that *I* depends on inner images that form the world you see, like a dream. Every time a thought arises, it is fictive, imaginary, dreamlike. Do you understand that all of this world is just a story?

If you are awake for a long time, you will come to learn what it is to be free from the world of images and thoughts, the dreamlike world of stories. But you may feel bored, uninterested, and empty. This is because you are not affected by any story. But this is not because you are awake, but because you are in the final chapter of your *story*, that is, the story had come to speak of emptiness, nothingness, meaninglessness, and uselessness.

You have to realize this is also part of the story. Emptiness, boredom, and lack of interest are part of the plot. In the state of being awake, emotion doesn't exist, as emotion is relatively caused by the happenings in a sort of story.

Emotions arise from stories. So get out of the story. The moment you do, you will experience a tasteless clarity and won't be able to find emotion, as it is the result of the phenomenon of exchanging energy with things divided into this and that.

Every time you experience something, it is absolutely certain that this experience includes the feeling of *I*. Even the feeling of *being*, although it's very subtle, includes the feeling of *I*. It is possible to experience even *nothingness*. However, you will become conscious of the experience of nothingness after it happens.

It is like a wave. Waves consist of troughs and crests. The presence of a crest is evidence of a trough. No matter how much you have experienced the feeling of "I do not exist," the *I* in this phrase means that *I* was there all along. Every experience is a wave that contains a trough (*I*) and crest (*object*). A crest cannot exist without a trough, and vice versa. They necessitate each other. In other words, an "I-You" experience means that your *I* has experienced a *thing that is not you*. However, some things are not an "I-You" experience. The height of waves decreases as you go further out to sea. And as there are no waves in the deep sea, there is no "I-You" in the depths of consciousness. A leap takes place there. You leap from the movement of the ocean—choppy or calm—to just *water*. There is just *water*. Once this leap occurs, you can come back to life and realize that the waves are also just water. No matter how high a wave, it still remains as water.

EXERCISE 26

If you cannot escape the feeling of emptiness, try to stay at the level of *subtle sensation* just below the surface of *I* and *you*. This is a place where there is always a delicate thrill of joy because there is no *subject* nor *object*. In other words, submerge yourself until you are right below the level that feels like reality. Using the human body as an example, this is like moving your focus from the level of organs identifying all the organs that are distinguishable from each other, to the level of cells that make up those organs.

The reason you feel empty is that you are used to being in a state of separation. If you can identify this level and find the level just below it where there is no separation, you do not have to stay in the world of separation. You only have to return to it when you need to. In the level where there is no separation, you will experience only the calm thrill of joy.

AWAKENMENT PRACTICE

We are now ready to move on to another dimension. It is time to go beyond the level of thought and realize that we are bigger than thoughts. Many people preach this nowadays, but all this proves is that we are all immersed in thought all the time. Just as thoughts and imagination create our physical reality, a more fundamental sense of presence creates these thoughts. We are now entering a world in which the sense of presence creates thoughts. Like a toddler stumbling upon taking their first steps, you may be clumsy at first, but you will soon move beyond the headspace of an awkward beginner and step to the dimension in which you can gain total control over thoughts.

Instead of settling for the state in which we can experience silence, enter a meditative state, and feel cosmic fullness, we will try to move beyond it. In other words, you will realize that you are both the one that experiences all these things and a transparent *being* that is not experienced. Furthermore, we will understand that everything in the world is the source, which manifests so that we can enjoy *using* everything we have experienced—our goal. Then we will observe thoughts with no attachment and not belong to any separated group.

Awakenment Practice

Awakenment means staying at the source. I have already said that the source is timeless and absolute inexistence. There is no separate *being* in the source, so it is not something that can be experienced.

The nature of consciousness is the background between individual thoughts against which thoughts occur, and the source secretly bears both of them. Therefore, it is a place that can never be *known* nor *felt* by *anyone*. As our term for it suggests, it is the very source of everything that happens to us. Some people say to look between your thoughts to find it. But if you can find it there, it is not the source. If you can see it, it is not the source. You can be the source and make all other thoughts and feelings possible, but you cannot experience the source. If you experience frustration on your journey to find the source, it is because you are trying to figure out something that is by nature unknown and unseen. Just as eyes cannot see themselves and scissors cannot cut themselves, we can never see our source. Nevertheless, there is a way to confirm that it is there. Of course, this method is new and completely different from the usual way we go about achieving knowledge. I think this is why it is said to be so difficult to know the source. As a matter of fact, the source of our consciousness is always being *used* to know something else. Without it, we could never know, see, or hear anything. Once you realize this, you can never say you do not know it, and you should realize how absurd it would be to say that you do not know or cannot know it.

In other words, the source is not something that exists. Therefore, it cannot be experienced. Existence comes from being separated. How can you say something that is not separated exists? For example, look at the sea. When it is still, only the sea exists, but when the wind blows and waves rise up out of the sea, the waves exist, too. Only then the waves can be seen, known, and experienced by the sea. Like so, that something exists means that it is separated. Only then it can be recognized.

Since the source, which makes everything possible, is not separated from anything, there is nothing that can be said to *exist*. So how can we recognize what does not exist when what we can experience and recognize is limited to what exists? What cannot be the object of experience and awareness cannot exist, either. Thus, we cannot be *conscious* of the source's existence. However, it is not that it does not exist altogether, nor is it that it exists despite these limitations. It is beyond concept itself. It is the basis of all consciousness, including pure consciousness. So, to put it into words, it is ultimate nonbeing. It is not *existent* but it is the basis of the existence of all consciousness, the first of which is *taiji*. In order for something to be experienced, polarity is necessary. Pure consciousness also has a subtle polarity. For this reason, there are people who say they have experienced pure consciousness. There is consciousness that has no content but still can be experienced. We will call it *taiji* consciousness. It is this *taiji* consciousness that we can experience by being awake. It has a subtle hidden polarity. That means you can experience it. This cannot be truly expressed in words, but to try, it can be said that it has a *polarity that simultaneously does and does not exist.* This is why I have expressed it as *experiencing the inexistence of I through traces of one's self* in the second stage of being awake. In other words, it is experiencing something through *traces* that appear to be real but are not. By fully experiencing *taiji* consciousness, you can now use it as the basis for knowing (indirectly) the ultimate nonbeing that is the source.

To Realize the Nature of Consciousness

Ever since you are awake, you become wiser and sense the occasional break from identification. But your center of existence remains in thought, which you do not realize is an object itself. This is because you have learned that everything that appears is an object, but, having lived so long *identifying with what's been experienced,* have not made this final recognition.

This last recognition is that you notice that everything that you touch, feel, or know, without exception, is an *object.* What is left once you make this final realization? When you cross this threshold, the essence of consciousness called true self, or transcendental ego, is finally revealed.

• To Return to The Radiant State Without Any Object

This is like returning to one's original place. After experiencing the last experience of being that is *taiji*, practice returning to your *original place* immediately after you experience any given object. This place has no content, no taste, no color, and no touch, not even faint ones. Of course, there is no smell or fragrance, either. There are no thoughts, emotions, or feelings. The final feeling you can ever experience in this place is *taiji* consciousness, what occurs when you subtract everything from *being present*. As demonstrated in the analogy of the keyboard, it is the state in which you can reach any key at any time, but are not touching any, and leave no traces of attachment on the key you just pressed. You in this state can experience anything clearly and accurately, without being disrupted by thoughts or emotions. After every experience, you can return immediately. After returning, you leave no traces of attachment on the keyboard.

This place is a transparent light and an infinite, unrestricted mind. There is neither the idea nor the feeling of *I*, thus, there is no limitations by *I*.

BEING AWAKE TESTIMONIALS

Reading about being awake and actually experiencing it are two very different things, as evidenced by the following testimonials. Please read them and practice the exercises in this book to understand for yourself.

The Boundary between Thought and Feeling

Cheongang
entrepreneur and Holos promoter

This article, originating from Cheongang's presentation to the members of the Thursday Gathering, recounts his experience completing the first level of the Being Awake program that was held for several days starting on November 30th.

Before I sent that e-mail to you all, members of the Thursday Gathering, I rewrote it a few times. The first e-mail I wrote went like this: "Ah! This is the result I have been seeking for 20 years." But, upon rereading it, I felt it was too much, so I tried to write it again. I tried to highlight the result I wanted to convey, but my explanations seemed to be just a random collection of letters, and my writing about my experiences did not achieve the effect I'd hoped it would. The experience I'd had this time was definitely different from those I'd had before, but what was the difference? There was no way to explain it. So, I thought there was no other way to communicate it to you all than to let you to experience it yourselves.

Last November, on the sixth day of our log cabin stay to experience the program guided by Wolin, I had a momentary vision. It was just going into some unknown place. While I was inside it, I was not able to remember the time at which I had been outside. I was not able to find the door. I left it and tried to find which door I went through, but still could not find it. It just happened by itself.

Then what happened to me and what changed? Usually, after going to training workshops, I feel like I almost go crazy. How should I say this? It felt like my voice changed. My voice changed drastically. I used to think that my voice was enough to convey the excitement of an experience to another person, and if the person was not excited, I would actively try to make him or her excited. This was something that I did. However, after I came back from the workshop, I talked with a few people and I felt like my voice had ceased to work in that way. Why was this? In the past, since I was able to explain things in words, I was able to instruct you all. But now it was more imperative that you not listen, but experience for yourselves. Rather than saying I experienced something, it would be better to say I saw a certain state. After seeing it, I cannot go back to a time in the past in which I have not seen it.

The ordinary mind is what I have aimed for ever since I started doing consciousness training. The ordinary mind is the way, and the way is realized in everyday life. This means that no matter how valuable a momentary experience is, if you do not maintain it when you return to daily life, it is meaningless. It is as if one day, putting on your pants, you asked yourself if you put in your right or left foot first. You don't remember the answer. In my case, however, I do not even try to notice which foot goes first; it is just seen. This means that I can see which leg goes first every time I put on my pants. I simply notice it, like, "Oh! My left foot went first." I would say that the flows of actions, experiences, and thoughts can all be felt at the same time.

So, how does this help you in reality? For example, when I speak, I can hear my voice, which I am talking about. Before, I was able to hear it only when I was conscious of it, focusing on it. Now, it comes natural for me to recognize and listen to something. Now that the field of my vision is broader, I can see all of your facial expressions and at the same time hear my voice. I can hear the mechanical sounds coming from this projector, too. I am speaking, but I am also feeling that my voice is crackling. Still, I never lose the context of the story. Because it is not that I speak by following my thoughts; rather, the words just come to mind. Thoughts should not drag you.

After experiencing this, I realized that we can never achieve skills like listening and empathy just through effort. They just appear on their own. Now, when I look at someone, even though I do not make any effort, it seems like a name tag attached to the person is detached.

A few days after I realized this, my son called me. These days, he is very happy because he was accepted into the Seoul Institute of the Arts. He told me that he talks to himself often, things like, "I cannot believe that this is real!" and that he also hasn't been able to stop smiling because he had never believed that he would be able to enter the college. Not so long ago, he did a graduation performance. It was a high school production that took place right after he had been accepted into the college and he performed with a boost of confidence. Much of the audience was surprised, some even saying that he looked like a real actor. Some older women approached him for autographs. A foreign woman told him "I performed Grease in the US, but while I was watching you play the character, I think I misread it. I think I learned from you."

That was the highest compliment he had ever received. When he told his mother about it, she was so happy that she could not stop smiling and telling me about it. But, at the moment, while I was looking at her face, I felt like I was seeing holes, round and black, white, and brown. It looked like the holes next to each other just went back and forth, and there was a mouth gaping open below. I couldn't recognize her smiling face that was smiling as a face at all—I was looking at something without judgment. I thought this over. What was this state that I had entered? I thought it seemed similar to a newborn seeing the faces of her parents and other people for the first time. This lack of judgement means that when you see an object, stories or names associated with it do not come to mind. Instead, you just see it as it is.

At that moment, I asked myself, "Your wife and your child are so happy, so why is your mind not dancing?" But when I stepped back and looked at my mind, this question disappeared. I realized with a start that my mind was not mine after all. Does that mean that if I lose my mind, I cannot feel emotional? "wow, great!" If it goes like this, there are emotions mixed together. I am embarrassed to say this now. I mean, it is not natural to feel so excited about something like that. The next thing that came to my mind was creation. In the Bible, in the beginning, there was chaos. Chaos stopped and left behind the heavens, earth, and everything else in existence. God created animals, plants, and human beings, and saw that they were good. I feel like this line, "God saw that it was good," does not mean that it was beautiful, but that it was simply "as it was." It feels like everything is exactly the way it was made. There is no judgement and distinction. So, who is the one who creates? It is not God, but human beings. What did God say to Adam? God told him to give names to all creatures. That is creation.

While I was going through this experience, I happened to see several types of clocks on the wall. But, when I called one a clock, the thing on the wall said, "Um, I am not a clock!" It made me think about if what I was seeing really was a clock. The shape was different from all the others. At that moment, I realized that names are used for the purpose of communication, and I need names to put labels on things. That was the way Native Americans did it.

The Sunday after this happened, I met up with Y. He was initially really worried about me, thinking, "He has been hanging out with Wolin and doing things like Tao practice. He must be finally going on his way. What about his business? What should I do?" As soon as we met, he asked me directly, "All right, I understand, but does this have anything to do with your business?" In fact, I asked myself the same question on the sixth day of the training workshop. On that day, I was feeling like I was making progress, and I think it's fair to say that my consciousness had expanded. "What is the relationship between the expansion of my consciousness and the way I live my daily life?" I asked myself. "How will it help me in the business field, specifically?" But it turned out to be very helpful. At the moment, what came to mind was that I could improve my listening and empathy. However, we cannot improve these skills just by trying hard. Actually, I once participated in an intensive program called Awakening for 72 hours in Minaisa that focused on listening and empathy. In the program, we did nothing but pour our hearts and souls into listening and talking, looking each other in the eyes for 72 hours. It was a totally new experience of listening, one I had never had before. And it took effort. You have to put effort into being conscious.

But now, for me, consciousness is a phenomenon that happens by itself. The reason this is possible is because my mind is not attracted to nor blindly follows my actions. Thoughts do not simply arise anymore because the mind has disappeared. My mind is something I use when I need it, not something that belongs to me. Thoughts are necessary tools that I use when I use my mind, not things that are inside me. This is not something that can be explained in words, so I decided to come up with a way to help you experience it yourself.

However, while I was preparing these exercises, they didn't work when I got people to try them out. While I had, over four days, been talking about how "I feel confident about these exercises. They are really easy," they did not work out. It was then that I realized that it is quite difficult to help others find and enter the door that one has already entered, because it happens in a flash. A member of ours who went to a program said that they saw something. In the meantime, since I have also run several programs, I think this is possible. But, in order to make it easy for someone to experience or understand it, you have to stop them at the exact moment that they see it, saying, "Try again. Rewind and rewind." You must make sure that they can clearly recognize what the exact point is. That way, they can easily find the doorknob and show them the way. For example, let us say that someone takes you to a huge theme park. When you try to leave, you cannot find the exit. No matter how hard you try to find it, you cannot, because someone guided you into the park. It is like the phenomenon of people who do not drive not being able to identify a route they took by car.

For most of my life, it was not me who had been driving my life, but my thoughts. I wasn't able to find the critical moment, the point at which one stops directly in front of the door, because my thoughts were my guide. Therefore, you must stop when you get into that point, and the rest is training until you get used to it and become able to freely enter and exit the door there. My goal was to figure out how to help others see this easily and quickly. Even Wolin, who guided this program, told me that some people can make it work and some cannot. The reason that some people cannot is because they are not able to "find the doorknob," as I put it. However, it was almost at the bottom, so I had to guess vaguely, feeling around and guessing, "This must be it!" It is said that at the door, there two more steps left, the step where there is no need to put in further effort and the step where you see that the state of being awake and the state of sleeping are the same. I suggested that we let the members of our meeting experience being awake in everyday life, just like I had experienced. That is why I stopped there.

What I felt as I came here was "Ah! I finally, I get to experience it here after 20 years." What bothered me the most was that I was still burdened by thoughts, which meant that I was under the control of thoughts, circumstances, and phenomena as I become more and more sensitive. But now, the reason I am not swayed by these is because the focus of my consciousness is not on thoughts but on the base of them. So, what I want you to experience today is what is at the base of thoughts.

......

It is a feeling. It is not a feeling colored by emotion or sentiment but belongs to the world of pure sensation or feeling that exists before this coloring occurs. Creation does not come from thought, but from feelings. Feelings and thoughts are connected. When I'm in the dimension of feeling, thoughts cannot randomly approach me. So, it is necessary to focus on the question of how to enter the world of feeling. The focus of your consciousness should not be drawn to thoughts or phenomena, but to the feeling that occurs first. Where should you start searching for feelings? Just awaken the five senses of touch, taste, sight (*sigak* in Korean) etc. Take a look. *Si* means seeing. *Gak* means awakening. Likewise, it symbolizes that the senses of taste and touch can reach *gak* through gustatory and tactile sensation. That way they can awaken. I once thought that the way to become awake could be found in training sessions, Bible studies, or meditation practices, but now I feel like the reason these did not work is because they were unfocused. Focus can be manifested through training the five senses. After I realized this, I thought that artists must be people who are on the verge of being awake. Think about it. When post-Impressionists like Van Gogh and Renoir made their paintings, how could they describe a tree with fiery branches when they didn't have it in front of their eyes? Give it a try. Can you look at a tree for an hour or two without thinking of something else? They probably looked at trees for about 10 days at a time, not one or two hours. In this amount of time, the pine tree disappears and only 'it' remains; to put 'it' into words, it's a feeling. To express 'it' with color, they do this and that until what they saw is properly described. What is this about? It means that only the ones who can see are able to draw and create.

Shall we talk about listening? I always listen to classical music radio stations in the car. Usually, I only listen to the songs I know and when other songs play, my attention drifts. When we hear songs that we are very familiar with, like "Dancing Queen" by ABBA, which many of us listened to often when we were young, at the moment, what happens? Your attention goes to your brain. The brain recalls the memories and emotions that are associated with the song, and they rise to the surface. So our bodies react. But now, I hear it as just another sound. The more sensitive I am to the sound, the fresher and more interesting it seems, but does not come together as a melody. In the case of the drum sounds in the song, they all sound different. Some sound big and some sound small. Furthermore, I also hear the radio DJ's voice without registering it as language. I am like a newborn baby hearing things. What is the reason that we often do not have a lot on our mind when we go abroad? It is because we do not understand what people are talking about. We can hear the sound of people talking, but our consciousness is not attracted to their speech. Listening to things as sound is similar to that. It is not that we distinguish between sounds, like, "This is a violin sound" or "That is a cello sound," but... Well, I cannot express it well, but if I had to try, it seems to be true that the world is just before language. Sometimes sounds are represented by lines. For example, if we ask children who understand the meaning of words to express sounds, they might draw a thin line when listening to a violin and a thick line when listening to a cello.

When you hear exciting music, you dance and groove. This does not happen by itself, necessarily—it is learned. If you are awake, even your most favorite song cannot excite you. It just flows through you. Another interesting thing is that when it passes, you won't remember it. You don't think about the future, either. Only through this phenomenon did I realize what the phrase "Here and now" means. It's not proper to call this an "understanding." though. Can you imagine it?

What I am talking about is that the key to being awake is where your conscious attention is. Let us try it now. Close your eyes and touch anything in front of you with your hands. A desk, a ballpoint pen, a paper cup—anything will do. If you touch something with your palm, try it again with your fingertips. Put your index finger on the object you have just touched and focus your consciousness on the point where your fingertip is touching the object. Now, open your eyes. There is a difference between when you touch it with your palm and with your fingertip, right? Let's try it again. Try to hold an object, touch the floor, or hold the ballpoint pen. We know what a ballpoint pen is, but it is not about knowing it. Just close your eyes and touch it with your fingertips. Whether it is something you know or not, focus on the feeling of the object in your hand. It is okay to move it around to try to find this feeling. Try to separate how much of what you feel is thought and how much is feeling. This is the first step toward finding clues.

(*Audience member speaks.*) "It felt tough and cumbersome. But when I touched it with my fingertip, it felt simple. That is the difference."

You said it was tough and cumbersome. Are those feelings?

"I think cumbersome is a feeling and tough is a thought."

You said that it felt "simple" when you touched it with your fingertip, but out of your three descriptors, which one would be the closest to a feeling?

"Cumbersome. Well, I think it is more like a thought than a feeling."

Right. Now you are on your way to finding the answer. Actually, feelings like "cumbersome" or "tough" are more like thoughts. It is not the object that is cumbersome or tough, but your thoughts that say they are. What you need to recognize is that thoughts include emotions as well as judgement and everything else that composes us.

Feelings exist right underneath all of our thoughts. Only when you find them can you enter the world of feelings. What is the world of feelings? It is a pre-language world. The first thing I noticed during training was that I was always sleepy. Whenever I was told to feel something, I ended up thinking about other things and would nod off. I had never nodded off during these kinds of trainings before—quite the contrary—I could never fall asleep. How could I fall asleep in classes where I should keep using my brain and mental energy to learn something? But this time, I actually did quite a lot in the beginning. I thought of Mr. Y, a member of the Thursday Gathering, and suddenly understood why he often nodded off during training. What is the reason? I think it happens when we cannot find a contact point between thoughts and feelings. I have a lot of thoughts, but no feelings. I feel like the word "thought" itself is personally hard to understand. Mr. Y, on the other hand, has lots of feelings, but doesn't have enough words to express them. As if he were playing Tetris, he goes back and forth to find proper words for his feelings, which makes him doze off in the end. It's admirable in a sense that he has that many feelings. I think since there are a lot of feelings inside him, it must be very hard for him to organize his abundant feelings into thoughts.

I thought that this phenomenon not only demonstrates how limited our modern education and communication systems are, but also prevents creation. If people start painting or making sculptures to express themselves, their lives will change. For me, maybe I would have been doing installation art like Nam June Paik instead of business. (*Laughs.*) I have talked about the distinction between thoughts and feelings for a while, so, is there anyone who can tell how much space thoughts take up and how much space feelings take up? Could you tell us about that? Mr. J, what percentage do you think, for thoughts and feelings respectively?

"Things seem to become thoughts the moment when they are expressed in language."

You're getting closer. I think you're getting the hang of it through this discussion. I tried it in the bathroom once. I ran cold water and hot water over my palms and fingertips, trying to sense it. When your fingertip is just barely touching the water, you cannot feel the difference unless you are awake. Then, you move on to consciousness. Cold? Who taught you that it is cold? Where did the word "cold" come from? The same goes for water. Who taught you that it is water? Try it out when you go home, everyone. You have to reach this by yourself. It is just like grabbing a doorknob. Everything we have tried so far has been using the sense of touch. Now, let us try something with sight. (*Shows an object.*) What do you think this is? Raise your hand if you have never seen this before. You guys are seeing it for the first time, right? What do you think?

"......"

Just now, one of you looked around at the others and said, "It is like something." This means that you used the sense of sight. Is the sentence "It is like something" a thought or a feeling here? I am giving you a hint right now. Let me show you again. Take a look at this. (*Shows something.*) There was something in the air just now.

Your brain starts working to figure out what it is, but you do not know because it has never existed on Earth before. How do I know this? Right now, I feel like I am a primitive man or an alien. This is the first step of feelings. We experience these kinds of situations countless times in our lives. The key of this story is that feeling indicates the state just before thought. Mr. J said, "They are just beyond words." This is right. The fact that they cannot be described in words means that they are all different for every person. When someone really catches a glimpse of the world of feelings, with the right stimuli at the right time, the world of feelings will wide open for them. That's what happened to me.

I tried experiencing things with my sense of touch while in the bath. I touched my skin, either in the bath or shower, and realized that after I had lathered on soap, it felt totally different. If you sense everything singularly, starting from things like splashing water on your body, a new world will soon open up to you. In the world of thought, we judge by inference and can lose interest by entering a boring, systematic world, but the world of feeling is infinite and endless.

After that, I tried again with food. I ate spicy stir-fried octopus with rice, which actually, until recently, had been my favorite food, but I suddenly felt pain. Oh! Spiciness is actually pain, not a taste, I realized. Also, when I ate bean sprouts or rice, I was not able to tell the difference because I possessed no judgement. I did not even close my eyes when I ate, but if you were to ask me, I would say that they were bland. Let me give you another example. I ate two rice cakes and some tofu this morning. I also ate a pear. The tofu was bland. Of course, it tasted as it normally does, what we call a savory taste. But no, I do not think there is such a taste. Since I go to a gym these days, I just interpreted it as protein. After that, I ate a seasoned rice cake. It seemed to have salt and sugar, because it was salty and sweet. In the past, when judging the overall taste of the food, a kind of a standard was always present, helping me understand if it was familiar or not. Since the standard had disappeared, I felt like I could discern a food's raw materials and notice subtle differences in flavor. So, when I have food now, I do not feel things like "good" or "delicious." The expression "delicious" is actually an interpreted emotion, not a feeling as it is. It is a clear example that sensing flavors means that you are familiar with them. Tasting wine is kind of a trend these days, so, if you try it, you will know what I'm talking about. Just take a look at explanations of wine regardless of quality. The wine descriptions in the manga called *The Drops of God* are sort of like paintings. No matter how much wine I try, it does not taste like it is described in the book. So, I don't understand the author. What I mean is that the sense of taste is always under the influence of your previous experiences. So, can change happen there? Whether you all here are for business or not, in the future, when creativity will be of utmost importance, what you need in order to awaken is the use of your senses, especially the five physical ones. For sommeliers, it is important to be very sensitive when it comes to wine, but I feel like we do not need to do that. If you are in a state of mind that can discern tastes, stir-fried octopus with rice is still good. However, if you are awake, there is no such thing as standard taste. Everything is flavorless. You just feel a subtle difference between them. This led me to feel like I couldn't remember the tastes of things. It was a little difficult. How do you feel about this? Sometimes you know, and sometimes you don't.

Now, we have just seen this thing that we have never seen before. At the moment there were a lot of things going on in our minds. Why is this? Because we were trying to define it. In other words, it can be said that feeling is what comes immediately before the motion to define. When I see something, it touches my heart. It really strikes a chord with me. But then, "Hey! It looks like chocolate," becomes a thought in my mind. Do you understand? It suddenly appears. But if our level of consciousness and thinking was the same as children's and these thoughts didn't arise, what would happen?

......

What do you usually find yourself looking for? We often unknowingly follow the things that are related to ourselves, thus getting closer to ourselves. But why do we do this? It just makes us dwell in stories and memory. But since the here and now is not a story, we just pass it by. Being awake means that you can see everything with and without stories, as necessary, and see things with and without names, as necessary.

Now that I have experienced being awake, when people come to me with requests like, "Let's do something," or "We need to do something," since I have no judgement, I don't experience any feelings. For example, when, in the past I had to meet and talk with people I really did not like, I would have thoughts like, " I do not want to be embarrassed," and "Do I have to do this at my age?" "Am I willing to go through this just to make some extra money?" However, now when I have to do something, I just do it. I am the background. A clean slate. For example, let me compare myself to the Microsoft Windows operating system. Windows can only work if you install programs on it. Similarly, I do not move unless I am told to. Without being captivated by thoughts, I just do the actions that I am commanded to do. Anyway, the most precious thing was learning that I am not my thoughts. Actually we have already realized this consciously through numerous practices. However, after originally believing that thoughts and identity are derived from things like one's parents, when I went a step lower, I found a world where thoughts do not arise. I am telling you that I have seen and experienced such a world.

This is the first step. When you recognize what comes before thoughts, please come and talk to me about it. I will try to guide you to the next level of training.

Now, I am going to show you seven pictures. Please look at them carefully. There is a boundary between thoughts and feelings. Look at each picture and determine where the boundary is. (*Shows pictures one by one.*) Do you know what this is? It is a rare pine tree on *Songnisan* Mountain. People who are familiar with this imagery will immediately identify this as a pine tree in the mountains. They fall into it before they even realize that they have. The same goes for this photo (a *hanok*, or Korean traditional house). In other words, you skip the process of feeling the image. But what happens when you see it as it is? It feels like when you read a text without absorbing its content. For example, you might read the phrase, "fire hazard," but instead understanding that it means you should be careful, you only see the individual letters. If you are awake, you can see it like that.

This is a brick, and that is a letter or character. Before it was called a letter, it was a line of black ink. and before that, it was nothing in particular at all. The state of being awake means that thoughts like, "This is a *hanok*" do not arise and we just feel things as they appear. But when we look at this picture (*shows an abstract picture*), we don't have any basis upon which to form a thought. So, we try to define it using the information that is already in our minds. But as we try to search for this information, the thought usually ends up dying out due to lack of interest. We are not interested in things we do not know. In this case, to what extent is it a feeling? Think about it. I think this is a difficult one. Just take a look at this picture. If you look at this in the state of being awake, you do not make automatic associations like, "This is a tank," or "I want to ride it." Those are feelings. When something comes to you, you experience a moment of realization and things start working. Now, let us look at the final photo to really see the contrast between feelings and thoughts. Here is a zebra, and here is a white screen. There is no difference between these two things. When judgement, discernment, and stories disappear, we can find an entrance into being awake.

Well, what I can give you right now is a doorknob. There are countless doorknobs. We do not know through what sense you will find the correct doorknob. So, as one of my teachers once reiterated in a lecture, it is essential that our eyes, ears, and nose are opened. I could not understand that at the time. I thought that it was just a typical phrase: "Keep your eyes and ears open." But now that my eyes are literally opened, I understand what it means. I can really hear sounds. I never thought that it was possible to hear them like this. Right now, I can hear this projector's fan running while I am talking. When we pay attention to one thing, we usually cannot hear or sense others. But right now, even as I focus on speaking, I can hear everything.

In the state of being awake, there is no distinction between you and me. Usually, in our religious and spiritual lives, we constantly try to follow a path that we think we need to take all the way to the end with a strong will. But that shouldn't be the only way. It's like taking the long way around. This is why many people deny what they have experienced and deny that Jesus came. It is an ongoing phenomenon in human history.

Lastly, before we wrap up here, let us look at these pictures again and try to distinguish between feelings and thoughts once more. Take a look at this photo. Is it complicated? Feelings and thoughts coexist here. Take your time looking at these pictures from the beginning again...

(Shows an empty screen.)

You have to empty your mind like this. Your *I* should go down below the level of consciousness. Although it is not a perfect analogy, let me give you one more example. From here, (*gestures to desk*) I can see all your faces. When I see one person, one thing comes to mind and when I see another person, another thing comes to mind. It is kind of complicated, but if I go down (*lowers head below the desk*) and do not rise to the surface, nothing occurs to me, because I cannot see anything. So, the key is where your attention is. In this example, above the desk means thoughts and below the desk means feelings. From the boundary between thoughts and feelings, you go down under the boundary, then you start to see things as feelings. Your eyes open. You do not even have to close them. (*Looking at a picture of a zebra.*) Newborn babies do not know this is a zebra. But, when adults look at this picture, they say it is a zebra. However, if you are awake, the word "zebra" is long gone, you just feel it directly. You experience no thought of "zebra," no thought of "tank," no thought of anything. You just stay in this state. Thank you. (*Applause.*)

Catching the Moment a Thought Arises

Hwadong
senior vice president of an SK subsidiary
Holos promoter

This article is a story of being awake through experience. It demonstrates that the moment you experience thoughts as feeling, you become free from them and that every experience keeps us away from experience itself.

I was lucky enough to participate in the Thursday Gathering's Being Awake training program, which started in January, through its third round. Although it is embarrassing to reveal that I have always been slow to grasp things, I decided to summon the courage to write down my experiences in the hope that it might be of some help to others who have questions about the Being Awake program.

In early winter last year, Wolin and Cheongang made an unexpected declaration after doing something somewhere. They declared that there seemed to be a way for everyone, even ordinary people, to reach enlightenment, and that they finally found the way.

For my whole life, although I had not yet lived very long, I had thought that enlightenment or spiritual awakening were accessible only to people in distant countries with special connections and preparations. I could never have dreamed of it for myself. I just lived with the belief that as an ordinary person, it was best to just work hard and have a good attitude. So I was half excited and half doubtful when I heard Cheongang confidently say that even ordinary people could experience enlightenment. Then, I eventually got a chance to participate in the Being Awake program held by Wolin in January of this year.

However, I spent my time as a participant worried, perhaps because I felt dull, and while the other participants seemed to gain something, I experienced little change as the hours of the program ticked away. On one hand, I was upset, and on the other, I was nervous.

Time passed, one day after another, until it was time for us to go back down into the world. (The training site was a log cabin in the mountains, so we literally had to go down the mountain to return to daily life.) It had ended, but I felt that I was leaving with no clear answers.

I returned home frustrated from the first training workshop. I was discouraged and felt wronged, angrily asking myself why I had failed, reluctant to accept my defeat. So, after the first workshop, I went home and decided to spend my early mornings at the university campus near my house in search of the feeling I couldn't find during the Being Awake training.

On the first day, time passed without any progress, and, having to go to work, I had no choice but to stop and leave it for the next day. The next day, like the day before, I went to the campus around dawn and continued to practice the boundary exercise, looking at the landscaped stones along the road and the shrubs planted in between them. At some point I experienced the phenomenon of the meaning of the objects becoming blurred.

"Ah! I'm finally starting to achieve something!"

Overwhelmed with sudden joy, I wanted to continue practicing, but it was time to go to work, so I hurried home and prepared to start my day. On my way to work, I continued to practice, picking up where I had left off at the campus. I started to feel confident, practicing by continuing to look at things that came to my attention regardless of where I was—on the way to work or anywhere at all. Next, I decided to move on from objects and start practicing on letters. So I started looking at the signs on the street. It was very difficult to practice looking at letters, but over time, I felt myself progressing until I reached a stage in which I could look at letters without thinking of their meanings.

I continued to practice by myself. A month later, I participated in the second Being Awake workshop. However, I again did not feel the intense change of sensation that Cheongang reported, and I felt unclear about whether I was on the right track. I climbed down the mountain again in a hazy, confused state.

If I had said that I had not gained anything after participating in the workshop twice, others might have laughed at me, so I acted as if I was getting something, considering my internal and external circumstances. So, it was half my own willingness and half social pressure that made me continue to practice hard when I returned home.

Perhaps I was too self-righteous, exclusionary, and hot-tempered because my job, which I had been doing for a long time, involved nitpicking and pointing out the mistakes of others. I knew that I had a bad habit of not acknowledging others, too. I tried hard to fix it, but just ended up frustrated when I failed. Despite all this, after the Being Awake program, I found myself possessed of the ability to look into my mind, and this, I think, has been the biggest change. Every Saturday morning, I hike up a mountain with my wife. While hiking, we usually don't talk to each other, just focusing on climbing hard. Despite the exertion of my body, my head has little to do at those times, so I used to come up with something to keep my mind occupied. But the first weekend after the Being Awake training, I had a striking and marvelous experience while hiking. I captured the moment when the thoughts that my head had created appeared in my mind. It was like watching bamboo shoots rise from a bamboo field after rain has passed through. The feeling of thoughts arising... It was a marvelous and surprising first-time experience, and I talked about it proudly at the Thursday Gathering. Those who had already experienced it congratulated me with applause.

Little by little, I began to get used to looking further into my mind as I went through the slow and sticky process. I practiced looking into my mind whenever something bothering me came up. I realized at some point while practicing that feeling is felt in the chest and the belly, and thinking is done in the head, although I still don't know if this is just the way I personally experience them.

I also slowly made progress by attending the Thursday Gathering, talking about my experiences and hearing about other people's progress during Wolin's regular checkups.

As I kept looking into my mind, I suspected that I was focusing too much on the changes of my body. When I brought this concern to Wolin, he replied that it was alright as long as I was not focusing solely on the feeling of the body, but on the being that is conscious of feelings as well. I did not entirely understand this answer, and time went by.

Strangely, however, after this conversation, I felt that my symptoms of hanging on to my body fade away (this phenomenon happened a few additional times, and as it repeated, I even thought that it was as if some invisible hand were helping me with my training).

I continued to look at the subject of feelings: anger, hate, sadness and so on. One Thursday (Holos promoters met regularly in Minaisa every Thursday evening), we had a discussion on at what moment one felt *I* the most. During this discussion, I thought that *I* must be an action of the mind. From that day on, I searched ceaselessly for the definition of *I*. However, no matter how hard I looked, I could not find anything past that *I* must be part of the mind, and I became convinced that *I* was the name tag of the mind and the mind was the body of *I*.

In other words, I became aware that the thoughts that had accumulated over the course of my life had created a fictitious concept of *I*, and I now acted like an owner. I have not had hands-on experience as a real owner yet, but now I know for sure that the mind is not the fundamental *I*. The good thing about this change is that it became easier for me to escape the various feelings the mind creates: anger, hatred, and judgement of right and wrong. I became less swayed by the action of my mind, and gained the power to look at things more objectively.

As these understandings became clearer, so did the process of looking into my mind. And as I came to understand that what I believed was *I* was only an action of my mind, I realized what the old sages meant when they said one must escape identification with the body and mind. What has changed significantly through this process is that the psychological discomfort that plagued my mind has been significantly reduced. For example, the hatred or anger I might feel toward the driver of a car that suddenly cuts me off while driving or the resentment toward those who have made me angry have both gradually weakened by themselves. I have changed so much that I do not feel anger or resentment past a certain level.

In addition, there have been many changes in my attitude toward life. For example, I found myself becoming more accepting of human imperfection than I had been before, and because of this, came to accept the mistakes of others more readily. Also, I gained a sense of the ultimate goal of life being to experience love.

In the meantime, the third Being Awake training workshop was held, and I gladly participated because Wolin said that it would be good if former participants attended.

At the third meeting, I experienced relief in an unresolved part of my mind, which came to me like the action of the invisible hand that I mentioned earlier. My personal feelings of hatred and anger felt almost entirely resolved, all but for my anger and hatred in the name of social causes or justice, which were not easy for me to lose, even though I knew that those feelings were created by an imaginary standard in my own mind. During conversation times that were a part of the training, I talked with my partner, Woosim. Mysteriously, after this conversation, that last remaining part of my anger and hatred had significantly weakened. This made me think again about the invisible hand, which I brought up to Wolin. He said that it is a very natural phenomenon that results from the nature of thought being rootless, and that the inflow of energy into hatred and anger stops as you get consciously aware of such emotions.

Ah! That is why!

I am proud of myself for changing day by day, and I feel surprised that I am finally becoming mature at over 50 years old. Anyway, I can't help but appreciate the good luck of having found this chance to live a more meaningful and valuable life in the latter half of my life. Thank you.

Pure Sensation Wakes

Hwang Bihong
yoga teacher

This report speaks about the composure gained by applying "space mode" between various emotions that were considered obstacles.

Before the Workshop

Last weekend, I went to the Being Awake training program hosted by Holos for two nights and three days.

Cheongang introduced the course two weeks before it started, and from that point on I waited with great anticipation, because he had apparently completed the training in secret. Clearly, he was a changed person. His voice was quiet and his behavior was calm and careful. I became even more curious about his experience, not only for his appearance that had changed, but for his saying "this is what I have been looking for over the past 20 years!", after all those years of seeking to satisfy his curiosity and intellectual thirst by attending all kinds of training at home and abroad.

I listened to him share his experience for over two hours. However, it was unexpectedly difficult to understand. Although it felt like I was coming to realization, no matter how hard I listened, I understood nothing fully. Later, the only thing I could remember was that he showed me something that I hadn't grasped, asking

"What do you think?" Other people were there, too. I can only guess they felt the same as me.

Two weeks after the introduction, Cheongang and Wolin, who had guided him in the previous workshop, hosted the training. Four people, including me, attended it in a log cabin on a scenic mountainside for two nights and three days.

The First Day

On the day the workshop finally began, it was snowing as if the heaven was showering us with blessings. But soon it became the heaviest snow we had seen all winter. I became a bit worried that it would keep us from arriving safely, as the training was being hosted up in the mountains. However, I was so excited that I made up my mind to climb up on foot if necessary. So I went to the home of the head of the Thursday Gathering (his nickname is Meoseum) early to prepare.

Despite the heavy snow, we arrived at the bottom of the mountain with no trouble. And thanks to Cheongang's new Jeep, we arrived safely, albeit a little late, at his log cabin halfway up the mountain.

Because we arrived late, some attendees suggested we take a rest, but we decided to go straight into reviewing the instruction for the workshop and start basic training. Wolin led the first training, which, fortunately, I adapted to more quickly because I had experienced it before.

The night after the training, I had a very interesting dream. I have had countless dreams in my life, but in this one, I very vividly remember looking at my own dreaming self. It was like another, separate me who was awake, able to watch itself dreaming. It lasted until dawn, when I clearly heard the clock sound five o'clock. I was amazed with curiosity, but, thinking that I should get some sleep for the following day, slept for a couple more hours. I didn't feel tired at all the next day.

The Second Day

After such an interesting night, I came downstairs to see Baram and Hwadong having breakfast already. We had some time to enjoy the beautiful mountain in the morning before the workshop began, so I went out searching for the trail that would take me to the highest peak, which I had seen in the darkness the night before. I ran with my own gait. Stepping on untouched snow on an empty mountain made me feel quite excited. I got excited like a puppy, even rolling around in the snow. It was good.

In the morning training session, I felt like I knew a little bit about what my dream was about. The training focused on recognizing the boundaries between things and had us focus our consciousness, going back and forth between indoor and outdoor while following guidance. I had experienced this before, so I was starting to get the sense of what I should feel more easily. One unusual thing is that, although I had little appetite due to not much physical activity, I kept feeling hungry for some reason. I suppose it was tiring for me to continually focus on consciousness at that time.

On the second day, we went to a large supermarket nearby. I enjoyed it, I guess because I usually enjoy moving around. I was fascinated with the surroundings as if I were a soldier on leave from a military camp. And the training with the objects on the shelves was very fun. How come everything looked so delicious... I actually tried free tastings several times, and I also felt that I was becoming full even if I just looked instead of eating. And the things that attracted my consciousness happily ended up in my stomach.

We went back to the cabin at night to be guided through some practice before going to bed. Due to the nature of the workshop, we were instructed not to talk much. I found it much more interesting when I did some yoga poses that I enjoyed. I'm not entirely sure why—maybe it was because the room was comfortably warm and I had eaten well. On that day, my body and my movements felt new. I was able to sustain difficult movements longer than usual.

The Third Day

I didn't dream like I had the first night. But I woke up refreshed and went out for a morning "patrol."

It was a lot colder than the day before. I found the feeling of the cold air on my skin and the fog of my breathing when I was running unfamiliar. Then, I was guided to the last day's training.

The training that day was also very interesting. Actually, the program itself was a little boring, but it was overall fun because I started feeling a conscious change in myself. However, although it was fun, I struggled with drowsiness on the third day.

After the guidance there was a time for each to meditate. I went up to the second floor and sat on a chair, looking out the window as the sun shone on me. How happy my life was... It was morning, so the sun came straight to me, a pleasure that I hadn't been able to enjoy before. I really enjoyed my time then, thinking about how difficult it would be to experience this happiness again. The winter sunshine seemed to embrace me so warmly. I was so happy.

The main point of the third day was to notice the distance and space between feelings and thoughts. This training was not carried out in a standardized, one-size-fits-all way, but customized to fit each participant, so I found that each of us came out of it with different feelings and different experiences.

Differences after the Workshop, 1

In the first week after the workshop's two nights and three days of training, I noticed some changes in my life. Sometimes I experienced a state that I call "feeling mode."

The first change was that boredom was gone. In fact, feeling bored had been the biggest obstacle for me at that time. I found nothing fun and frequently suffered from a boredom that was only remedied by dwelling on old memories, so I was frustrated myself with this lethargic state. Riding the subway for long distances in Seoul had become a painful endeavor for me.

Before, I used to travel above ground, on a Harley-Davidson motorcycle that was not restricted by traffic, but nowadays I travel on foot or by public transportation such as the bus and subway, so I spend a lot of time in boring transit. To avoid boredom, I would listen to music or read books, but now, even without such artificial efforts, I notice that a lot of interesting things are always happening.

In the past, even when I listened to music or read a book in the subway, I would feel awkward, always trying to avoid other people's eyes. But now, when I sit down and look straight at the people in front of me, I feel as if I am watching a puppet show without sound. The boundaries between people, the boundaries of clothes and surrounding objects, which I find interesting, are all very clear to me.

So, I am able to get something of use out of riding the subway. Even though a subway is a public place, there are still some people who behave without any regard to others. Especially late in the evening, there are drunken people who stumble around, stinking up the place. There are people speak very loud on the phone, regardless of if there are other people around. At these times, I recall my training experiences and activate "distance space mode." What this is is focusing on the space between those obstacles and myself so that I am not emotionally affected. However, I still cannot hold this mode for very long, so I eventually return to the realm of thought, but I know that with a little effort, I can duck back under my thoughts to my feelings, and be safe there.

Another change I have noticed is that when I close my eyes, without anything in particular to think about, I can recognize that I am in a state of thought and watch my thoughts rise like bubbles in water. Before, I floundered in the water of thoughts, only recognizing that I was in a state of thought after opening my eyes and shaking my head.

Now, I can watch them until they disappear. So I watch them more, and eventually I feel like I am under the boundary where the thoughts arise. Now that I am speaking about it, it sounds like I had had some special experiences, but it is just that I have the ability to play with thoughts and feelings.

Another very useful change is that these days, I have found a new field of study with which I can exercise my will. Basically, I have to memorize multiple chapters of educational material. I've never been good at memorizing and haven't done it for quite a long time. Additionally, the content of the chapters is very new and unfamiliar, with many strange, difficult terms. I was working on this before I went to the workshop, but I was struggling so much that I couldn't even finish the first page. At last, I visited Meoseum, who has amazing memorization skills, to ask for advice. After that, I was able to memorize the first chapter in 15 minutes while riding the subway. Meoseum's guidance had a big influence, but thanks to the Being Awake training, I was also able to become aware that every time I had looked at the book, my mind had felt burdened and pulled away. Now aware of myself resisting against the book, I could push back with ease. With this experience, although I know it will not be very easy, I think I will be able to memorize as much as I can because my mind has stopped resisting and pushing away. It was, practically, very helpful.

Differences after the Workshop, 2

A few days ago, I went to a large event to give a congratulatory performance. I planned to express the vibration of the belly through a *daegeum* (a Korean traditional wind instrument made of bamboo) performance, followed by a *jangseonmu* dance, performed while holding the instrument. Standing behind the stage waiting for my turn, I felt that the whole atmosphere was very dry. So I felt tight, inflexible. Perhaps this is similar to tension, but I knew that it certainly was not emotional, but a resonance of the waves of energy coming from people in the place. The reason I thought this was that while I was waiting, I was reminded of a feeling that I had felt while expanding my mind at the Being Awake training—this was the same feeling. So I changed my performance in the moment, and asked the audience to applaud when I was introduced, laughing out loud. I felt the atmosphere lighten immediately.

I usually wear glasses because of my poor eyesight and so when I perform, I usually take off my glasses right before the performance and just go on stage without any special measures. Of course, I respond by instinct. When I stood in front of the audience and looked at them without my glasses on, I felt the boundaries between them even though I could not see them. I felt myself leisurely watching the people bobbing their heads and having fun.

I finally started to play the *daegeum*. Before, I'd had to consciously put myself into a song to be immersed in it, but at this time I naturally felt the movement of my fingers, the sound of air entering the bamboo and flowing through the hole, and the way

I was standing all at once. At the same time, I also thought "Oh! The sound should be better." I went on to perform *jangseonmu* (a dance that connects the movement of the belly and the movement of energy to the body). Originally, when doing this dance, I had been inducing myself into some kind of trance. But now I could hear the music, feel movement extend along my arm from my shoulder, think about how my body should move next, overlook the concentration of people in front of me, sense the distance between me and them, control the speed of my movements, and think about if the instrument and I had gotten close enough to appear as one. In short, the whole thing had become much more complicated than before. But despite this complicated situation, I felt a simple comfort that was not dragged down by the complexity.

On the Second Week

I experienced frequent changes in the past week, too, and I decided to continue to develop what I gained from the workshop. Now, I am working on reducing artificial effort. I feel like I know what the stage of "let it become" is, so I will keep working toward it.

The great thing about the practice of being awake is that it can be used in everyday life, even outside of the workshop. Many of the activities felt good while I was participating in them, but as soon as they were finished, the feeling floated away as if I had done nothing more than watching a good movie. But I often make time to practice them in my everyday life, and sometimes they even show up by themselves, helping me to organize my consciousness and look at and think about myself.

And above all, I think that this practice is a good tool for picking out those feelings of reluctance against things that are new as well as my duties and desires, and also to see things for what they are.

Finally, I want to thank Wolin and Cheongang for preparing and hosting the workshop, and also Baram, Hwadong, Meoseum for helping to expand my consciousness. I have no doubt that good things will keep on happening and we will be happy.

Being Awake
The Grand Anatomy of Consciousness

Published by Herenow System Publishing Co.
53-70, Hwangsan-gil, Seoha-myeon, Hamyang-gun,
Gyeongnam, 50004, Republic of Korea
Phone: +82-2-747-2261
Email: cpo@herenow.co.kr
Website: www.herenow.co.kr

ISBN 978-89-94139-26-5, 03190

Author	Wolin
Translator	Kal Yonghoon Kim
Publisher	Won Kyoo Lee
Copy editor	Sarah Berg, Yeonju Kim

The publication of this book was sponsored by:

Ahso	Insoo Choi
Byunghee Park	Jagong
Byungsuk Kang	Jeonghee Song
Chayeoun Lee	Jeonghee Hwang
Cheolhee Lee	Jeyeop Song
Chiha Park	Jinhong Choi
Choon-Koon Yoon	Jiyeon Lee
Daehyeok Moon	Joh Day
Devi Lee	Jongsoo Hong
Dharma	Kibo
Dongin Jang	Kyung-Ah Lee
Eunhui Kim	Meekyung Youn
Eunju Min	Misuk Lee
Guehong Park	Myungjin Song
Gunwoo Lee	Namoo
Gyeonghee Seo	Sehee Hwang
Hado	Seonhee Yim
Hongsang Chung	Seungheon Kim
Hye Young Lee	Sungwon Yoon
Hyundong Shin	Wandoo Kim
Hyunho Lee	Yeongsun Oh
Il Heo	Younglae Park
Inho Jeong	and thirteen anonymous donors